The West Indies Federation

PERSPECTIVES ON A NEW NATION

American Geographical Society

Research Series Number 23

THE WEST INDIES
FEDERATION

Perspectives on a New Nation

EDITED BY DAVID LOWENTHAL

Published in Cooperation with
The American Geographical Society
and Carleton University
by Columbia University Press, New York
1961

The Authors

H. W. Springer, registrar, University College of the West Indies, Kingston, Jamaica.

Gordon Merrill, associate professor of geography, Carleton University, Ottawa, Canada.

Douglas C. Anglin, associate professor of political science, Carleton University, Ottawa, Canada.

David Lowenthal, research associate, American Geographical Society, New York, N.Y.

Preface

The birth of a new nation is the occasion on the one hand for celebration, and on the other hand for stocktaking, the analysis of strengths and weaknesses, and the definition of goals. The authors of these four essays serve the former purpose by contributing to the latter objective. Four scholars, three North Americans and a West Indian, here evaluate the past, examine the present, and ponder the future of The West Indies.

The portrait emerges of a nation somewhat unusual in the world community. Political independence is being gained after a long period of familiarity with political western ways. The economic development of The West Indies in the twentieth century is dependent upon capital assistance from abroad, although the level of production was relatively high in these islands over two hundred years ago. And by processes worthy of study the society of The West Indies has developed to the point where many races are living together in harmony. This is an accomplishment of no mean order, from which the world as a whole has something to learn.

These essays were originally presented as public lectures at Carleton University in Ottawa in April, 1959, with the assistance of The Canada Council. Although since revised for publication, they represent the views of the individual authors, rather than any general consensus. No good purpose is to be served by requiring conformity on matters where opinions honestly differ, and on several points of interpretation and policy these essays are at variance. Nor do they present a comprehensive picture of The West Indies. Nevertheless, as a group they will serve to introduce the general reader—not the West Indian expert—to the economic, political, and social background of these islands. The reader who wishes to go further into any aspect of West Indian life or landscape, past or present, will find guidance in the annotated reading list at the end of the volume.

The entire book has greatly benefited from the editorial services of Elisabeth L. Shoemaker, of Columbia University Press. The map appears here by courtesy of the *Geographical Review*, American Geographical Society.

Carleton University, Ottawa   GORDON MERRILL
May, 1960

Contents

The West Indies Federation

PERSPECTIVES ON A NEW NATION

BAHAMA IS.

CUBA

—20

Caicos Is.

Turks Is.

The Caymans

HAITI

DOM.
REPUBLIC

JAMAICA

—15

C A R I B B E A N

Aruba

—10

CANAL
ZONE

P A N A M A

COLOMBIA

V E

THE WEST INDIES

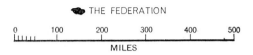

THE FEDERATION

0   100   200   300   400   500

MILES

The West Indies Emergent:

Problems and Prospects

H. W. SPRINGER

The problems of The West Indies are for the most part those of any country in transition from a predominantly agricultural economy to one in which a varied and expanding industrial sector may help provide a higher standard of living for a growing population. But there are, in addition, problems created by the fact of federation and by the peculiar geographical relationships and physical conditions of the federating territories.

The ten federating territories together comprise an area of eight thousand square miles with an estimated 1960 population of three and a quarter million people. But they are divided into two widely separated island groups—Jamaica in the western Caribbean with more than half the area and more than half the population, and the other nine units in a long chain a thousand miles to the east. Just as Jamaica predominates in the federation as a whole, Trinidad dominates the eastern group, exceeding all the remaining eight units together in size and population. Jamaica and Trinidad together contain 80 percent of the total land area and 78 percent of the total population. Together with Barbados, which contains 7.5

percent of the population on 2 percent of the land, these territories account for five sixths of both area and population. Mineral wealth is also unevenly distributed. Oil and asphalt in Trinidad and bauxite in Jamaica are the only valuable minerals known to exist in considerable quantity in the federation. The economies of the islands, however, have some common features. For example, they are all mainly agricultural, producing for export; sugar plays an important role nearly everywhere and is overwhelmingly important in St. Kitts, Antigua, and Barbados. In all the islands the ratio of labor to capital is high, unskilled labor is plentiful, and real incomes are low. All depend heavily on other countries for technical skill and capital.

The task of the West Indian statesman, in economic terms, is to make one economy out of these ten separate economies, which are at widely varying stages of development, with greatly unequal endowment of resources, separated by varying distances and by habits of independent action confirmed by centuries of practice. Moreover, this unity must be created without loss of momentum in the process of development now taking place, most noticeably in the larger islands.

Mention of "the West Indian statesman" recalls Plato's remark that metaphors from childbirth and shipbuilding suffice to illustrate all important truths. To use a metaphor from childbirth, the West Indian nation was born twenty years ago. The birth pangs began in the middle thirties, and the travail lasted for half a decade. To push the metaphor a little further, one might say that the period of gestation had lasted 100 years, conception having occurred with the final abolition of slavery in 1838. For it was then that the West Indians of today, descended from many races in Europe, Africa, India, China, and the Middle East, began to come into being as one people.

All who have known the West Indies before, during, and after the time of travail, 1934–39, would probably agree that the series of popular disturbances and riots which occurred throughout the British Caribbean during those years marked a turning point in our history. A tremendous upsurge of political energy characterized the period immediately following the disturbances. West Indians then threw themselves enthusiastically into the work of building a nation—organizing people into political parties and trade unions, and working for self-government, for a greater measure of social justice, and for a fairer share of the yield of agriculture and industry. It was then, too, that West Indians everywhere first began to accept themselves as West Indians. There was a new emancipation of mind and spirit. West Indian writers, painters, and sculptors began to produce works of art using West Indian themes and modes of expression; and West Indian music, dance, and folklore, formerly regarded as fit only for the amusement of children and nursemaids, began to be noticed and fostered with pride by the educated and the cultivated.

It would be hard to overestimate the profound change of outlook in this period. For the first time the people as a whole were politically awakened. In the context of each island's politics, the events of the 1930s could be termed a revolt of the masses against the plantocracy. But they were more. Throughout the islands, there was a movement for self-government and equality of status within the commonwealth; and the specific aim was usually West Indian federation with dominion status.

All this, while not strictly a part of my topic, yet is inseparable from it. For the enthusiasm for economic development which is to be found in The West Indies today is closely associated with the new national spirit. Indeed, the success of the efforts now being made to expand the economy will depend ultimately on the continuous enlistment of the support of West Indians at all levels of society.

The West Indies are, of course, not alone in this urge to combine independence and development with maximum speed. The British Commonwealth is well within its second great era of grants of self-government and autonomy, the first of which began a century and a quarter ago with the Durham Report in Canada and ended with the Act of Union for South Africa in 1910, and the second of which started after the Second World War. Cornelis de Kiewiet has contrasted the pace of events in the two periods:

We can be certain that history will not [now] permit a leisurely 80 years to be available [in the second period]. . . . Today political development is forced to follow a plan that substitutes years for decades, or more strongly minutes for hours. . . . Political change has forged ahead so fast that economics and education are labouring far behind. . . . That is why a new word has come to stand beside the old words self-government and autonomy. The new word is development. Once the slogan was "no taxation without representation," the slogan has come to be "no independence without development." [1]

W. Arthur Lewis makes substantially the same point in another way:

Peoples now in colonial status are anxious to become independent. Independent nations, numerous in population but poor in income, are anxious to have a higher status in the counsels of the nations. Rightly or wrongly, such people think that if they were richer they would count for more in international affairs, and there would be

---

[1] "American Education and the British Commonwealth," *Universities Quarterly*, XIII (No. 2, February, 1959), 132–33.

more respect for their nationals and for their way of life . . . most of the nationalists who have acquired power believe that it is necessary to have economic growth.[2]

This generalization certainly applies to the political leaders of The West Indies. Indeed, this may be said to be the one aim shared by all political parties.

II

Our West Indian statesman, as he looks around him, finds himself faced at the outset with a problem of population. The West Indies are overpopulated in the sense that a satisfactory standard of living cannot be provided for their inhabitants by agriculture and by existing secondary industries. If our statesman wishes to supplement the evidence of his own eyes with statistics, he will find that in 1954, when the income per head in the United Kingdom was about U.S. $860, the average for the West Indies as a whole was $235, with figures of $350 for comparatively rich Trinidad, $220 for Jamaica, $188 for Barbados, $128 for the Windwards, and $126 for the Leewards. There is no question of the need for economic growth in The West Indies. A better life for all is desired; it is even demanded as a democratic right. And a good life for all will require a considerable expansion of the economy, as the figures just given indicate. But the need is made especially urgent by the rapid rate of West Indian population increase. According to the West Indian demographer, George W. Roberts, the population of The West Indies is likely to double in twenty-five years.

There are several ways of dealing with the problem of over-

[2] *The Theory of Economic Growth* (London, 1955), pp. 423–24.

population. One is by controlling fertility. So far Barbados is the only West Indian government that has adopted family planning as an official policy. In some other government circles its importance is recognized, but it is not considered politic for the government to appear to lend assistance to such measures. Moreover, fertility control would in any case require considerable time to become effective; and so it can be of little influence at present or in the immediate future. Its potential importance in the long run, however, should not be underrated.

A second remedy is migration; and here the scope of the problem is a deciding factor. In the case of a country like India, for example, with a population of four hundred million, only migration on a massive scale could have an appreciable effect on population pressure; but in the case of The West Indies, with a population of three million, the emigration of a few tens of thousands may provide considerable relief. There are, of course, objections to emigration from the point of view of the national economy. In the first place, population is itself a resource. What is perhaps most likely to attract investors to set up secondary industries in our islands is a plentiful supply of labor at wages below those prevailing in the more highly industrialized countries. Secondly, a larger population is a larger potential market for the products of local industry. Thirdly, emigration tends to take away a high proportion of the more highly skilled members of the labor force, reducing the average level of efficiency. Emigration in excess of population increase can have highly deleterious effects.

A third remedy for overpopulation is the provision of new jobs at home. Our West Indian statesman fully realizes that agriculture is not likely to provide new jobs in the islands (except in the few areas where there is new land to be opened up). On the contrary, agriculture will probably provide fewer jobs as the years pass, while production continues to increase. In Barbados, for example, the estimated number of workers employed in the sugar industry in 1956 was 23,000, or only half as many as the 46,000 employed in 1881, when both population and sugar production were considerably less. Puerto Rican economic planners estimate that between 1955 and 1975 the number of workers employed in sugar production in that island will fall from 163,000 to 140,000. Meanwhile, the number employed in manufactures is expected to rise from 70,000 to 300,-000.[3] Agricultural production must of course be maintained, and indeed expanded; but greater efficiency will require new avenues of employment to take care of the excess labor now employed on the land.

Our statesman will not be unduly depressed by this, because he will have noticed that in recent years the level of West Indian national income, though low by comparison with that of more highly developed countries, has risen steadily, not withstanding the general increase in population. But he ought not give himself all the credit for this encouraging state of affairs. He should recall that for twenty-five years the West Indies have enjoyed unusually favorable conditions. Imperial and international trade agreements and price support schemes, beginning in the 1930s and augmented since the Second World War, have stabilized prices for the main export crops of The West Indies. In addition, partly owing to the general

[3] A. Mayne, comment in discussion of paper on "Employment Policy in an Underdeveloped Area," at Conference on Economic Development in Underdeveloped Countries, U.C.W.I., 1957, *Social and Economic Studies,* VII (No. 3, 1958), 68.

postwar expansion of the world economy, the West Indies have become less dependent on agriculture. The annual production of crude oil in Trinidad began to rise rapidly in 1950 and doubled within a decade. Bauxite production in Jamaica, which began in 1952, rose from 1,139,000 tons in 1953 to 5,722,000 tons in 1958. Oil and bauxite together now account for more than half the total value of West Indian exports. The tourist industry has also expanded rapidly since the war, especially in Jamaica, and is a source of much-needed income from abroad. This industry is also one which is most readily available to the smaller islands; in Barbados and Antigua tourist development has made notable progress. The past twenty-five years have also seen a substantial growth in manufacturing, chiefly in Trinidad and Jamaica, aided by active government support. These manufactures have been mainly for local consumption, but in the past few years the governments concerned have sought, with an encouraging measure of success, to attract overseas investment in industries manufacturing for export markets.

This attitude on the part of governments is in marked contrast to the policy which prevailed before the 1930s. In those days the spirit of national aspiration had not yet been born. And the instability of income, caused by fluctuating prices in an economy entirely dependent on export crops, dictated a financial policy of balanced budgets. Such reserves as existed were invested abroad. The favorable factors and conditions, together with the political events of the past three decades, have helped the policy-makers to change from caution, induced by chronic instability of income, to optimistic planning for steady and continuous economic expansion.

The rise in the national income during the postwar years has been general, but the rate of increase has not been as fast in the smaller islands as in Trinidad and Jamaica, a fact which is of great importance in connection with the unification of the West Indian economy. The tendency for the difference between the richer and the poorer units to grow wider suggests that the longer such practical measures of unification as customs union are delayed the more difficult they may be to achieve and apply.

Do these years of increased prosperity represent just another period of boom, such as the West Indies have known in the past, or have there been changes in the structure of the economy which will ensure the permanence of the current high levels of production and income? It is clear that no significant change of economic structure has taken place in the Windwards and Leewards, where agriculture is still the origin of 40 to 45 percent of the total income. Although Barbados has developed a variety of industries for local consumption as well as for export to neighboring islands, these are all on a small scale; Barbados still depends for survival on the proceeds of her sugar crop. The most striking changes in economic structure have occurred in Jamaica. A comparison of the figures showing in percentages the industrial origin of the Gross Domestic Product over the past twenty years reveals the degree of diversification that has taken place: [4]

	1938	1950	1956	1959
Agriculture	36.2	30.8	16.4	13.4
Mining			5.5	8.4
Manufacturing	6.5	11.3	13.2	12.9
Construction & Installation	3.5	7.6	12.7	11.4

[4] *The National Income of Jamaica 1956*, Table 3A, p. 48, and *Economic Survey, Jamaica 1959*, p. 7.

The mining, manufacturing, and construction sectors of the economy have all expanded at the expense of the agricultural. Though less preponderant, agricultural production, however, has in fact increased. In Trinidad oil exports are the largest source of income, and agriculture now accounts for only 12 percent of the Gross Domestic Product. The national income of Trinidad is probably rising even faster than that of Jamaica. For these two islands oil and bauxite may be expected to act as economic buffers, since they will probably be assured of a market and of reasonably stable prices, barring a severe or prolonged world depression. But in Jamaica agriculture occupies a sufficiently important place in the economy for a fall in agricultural exports to have serious repercussions. And even in Trinidad agriculture is still by far the largest single employer of labor.

On the whole, however, the economic structure of the major territories has altered profoundly. As George Cumper puts it:

We may conclude that the prosperity of the West Indies in the postwar years has involved some structural changes in the economy which appear to be part of a development process, that the possibilities of further changes in the same direction are far from being exhausted and that failing very unfavourable external events there is no reason why the area should not maintain a rate of economic growth sufficient to support an increasing population at a rising level of living for many years to come.[5]

III

I believe this optimism is justified. But it must be tempered with cautious realism. We have seen that a major factor in

[5] "The Development of the West Indies," in *The Economy of the West Indies,* ed. G. E. Cumper (Kingston, Jamaica, University College of The West Indies, Institute of Social and Economic Resources, 1960), p. 23.

recent prosperity has been the maintenance of stable prices for West Indian exports. Another factor has been the degree of protection these exports have enjoyed, partly through commonwealth preference, partly as a result of currency restriction, both of which have shielded them to some extent against competition from non-sterling sources. It is quite possible that the favorable conditions of the past twenty-five years will not continue indefinitely. There may before long be considerable relaxation of currency controls; when this takes place West Indian products will be deprived of some of the protection which they now enjoy. The coming into being of the European Common Market has made it less likely, if not impossible, that The West Indies can in the near future develop a sizable market for their products in western Europe. And it would be unrealistic not to recognize that West Indian independence, as well as the possible impact of the European Common Market, may result in a falling off of trade with the United Kingdom. West Indians are therefore thinking increasingly of expanding market opportunities in North America.

They are also concentrating more and more on North American investments. To take up the labor surplus The West Indies needs considerable outside capital in undertakings that will provide new jobs: in the hotel business, for example, and manufacturing. The West Indies welcomes investors from the United States and Canada who will produce in our islands goods for export to these and other countries. West Indian workmen employed in this way in increasing numbers, and enjoying a higher level of living, would in turn furnish an increasing market for imported products.

In short, general considerations of economic progress as well as special local circumstances lead to the conclusion that it will be to the advantage of The West Indies to encourage North American investment. Unfortunately, however, the islands which are least likely to attract investment capital are the smaller ones. They are also the ones that are most vulnerable to the vicissitudes of external trade. The effect of a disturbance in overseas markets for agricultural produce would be more severely felt in the smaller islands; and one of the effects of such a disturbance would be to widen still further the gap between the developing territories and the rest.

IV

The task before the West Indian statesman is to create a unified economy which will permit the smaller as well as the larger islands to share in the process of development: in other words, to make effective in economic terms the unity which has been created by law in the federal constitution. Customs union, together with its corollary, freedom of movement of persons, is the instrument necessary to achieve such unity. This fact was recognized by those who framed the federal constitution, the preamble to which states: (1) that "there should be the greatest possible freedom of movement for persons and goods within the Federation," and (2) that "it is essential for the economic strength of the area that there should be an integrated trade policy for the Federation and that there should be introduced . . . as far and as quickly as practicable a customs union including internal free trade." These objectives were given legal sanction in the constitution itself, and one of the first important federal acts was the appointment of a Trade and Tariffs Commission charged with planning a customs union. Their report was issued at the end of 1958 and its proposals are still being studied by the federal and unit governments.

As the commission report notes, Jamaica has been following a highly protectionist policy; should Jamaica have to abandon the use of quantitative restrictions as a means of implementing this policy she would need to employ higher tariffs in their place (though only for a limited time, since in the long run the comparative smallness of even the total West Indian market will require manufacturers to aim at markets abroad; they will have to pin their faith on efficiency rather than on protection). Trinidad, on the other hand, while embarking on considerable industrial development, has not employed protective measures to any great extent. But "just as this problem would have been easier to solve 5 or 10 years ago when this difference of interests, if it existed at all, was much less marked, so it will become more difficult if the Units continue upon different and divergent courses for another period of years." [6]

Once freedom of movement of persons, goods, and capital is realized within a unified customs area, the smaller islands will probably rely increasingly on supplying foodstuffs—fruit, vegetables, meat—to the larger islands, in turn providing an expanding market for their manufactures. The development of industry in two separate centers, Jamaica and Trinidad, will provide an element of healthy competition. Freedom of movement in practice means improved communication. Without the rapid development of air travel during and after the Second World War, the present type of federal association of The West Indies would not have been practicable. As the Trade and Tariffs Commission noted, "The West Indian situa-

[6] *Report of the Trade and Tariffs Commission W.I. W.I.* 1/58 § 66.

tion has been profoundly influenced in the direction of solidarity and community of feeling and opinion by the recent development of civil aviation." But more kinds of communication are required, otherwise contact "is not likely to go below the upper levels of intercourse. To create a West Indian nation and a West Indian economy the exchange of persons and goods by sea is necessary, and the improvement of shipping must go hand in hand with an active and growing demand for space both for passengers and for freight." [7] Improved shipping facilities are therefore of the first priority, and Canada has demonstrated her friendly interest by undertaking to build and present to The West Indies a pair of ships specially designed to meet the needs of the islands. Improved shipping facilities and expanding air transport will themselves be stimuli to production.

v

The question now is how the difficulties in the way of the unification of the West Indian economy may best and most quickly be overcome. The chief obstacles are: (1) the widely varying stages of development of the different islands, and (2) the unequal distribution of resources among the units. There is a further obstacle, in part psychological or political or both: the difficulty of overcoming separateness, bringing into being an effective customs union, and pooling resources. This difficulty is stated in its extreme form by David Lowenthal:

The problem of communication from island to island, and from islands to mainland, is not going to be solved soon, or easily. . . .

[7] *Ibid.* § 47.

As long as the separation of the territories is a physical fact, no category of resources can be pooled completely. Physical obstacles apart, none of the territories could afford to take for granted the pooling of resources . . . each partner in the federation must protect itself to some extent, use its own resources for itself, against the contingency that another territory might withdraw, or the federal structure collapse. Nor does political realism alone suggest such caution. In view of the distances and the uncertainties of weather and navigation, no territory can afford to merge all its resources with the rest; each must keep a measure of self-sufficiency as insurance against "natural" catastrophe.[8]

The risks of closer association are facts of our federal situation. But we have grown accustomed in modern times not to accept "physical facts" as permanent obstacles to desired goals. The problem to be solved is one of communications, and the progress that has been made in this direction in the last few decades makes it reasonable to expect that with time and perseverance the difficulty will progressively diminish. As to the need for a measure of self-sufficiency as a protection against natural catastrophe, this is not a serious obstacle. In times of calamity we all expect help from outside sources; modern communications make such help increasingly available. Finally, the fear of the failure of the federation itself must be met by a change of attitude. Nations are made when the sentiment for nationhood finds expression within the legal and physical framework of a state. The change of attitude will come with the sharing of the sentiment of nationhood. Time will show whether this national sentiment exists to the degree that is required to achieve lasting unity in The West Indies. I believe that it does. I believe that there is such a nationality as West Indian, created by common factors of racial origin,

[8] "Physical Resources," in *The Economy of the West Indies,* ed. G. E. Cumper, p. 55.

history, language, culture, and association, and that, not withstanding local differences, the West Indian is distinct from other peoples.

To quote Cumper once again:

Successful development will of course involve many problems of economic and social policy and of public finance. . . . The recognition that these problems are in principle soluble and that long-term development is a real possibility would appear to be a new and itself important factor in the history of the West Indian economy.[9]

[9] "The Development of the West Indies," in *The Economy of the West Indies,* ed. Cumper, p. 23.

The Survival of the Past

in The West Indies

For West Indians, as for many millions of other people, the twentieth century has quickened hopes for a better life. Formal political independence, now virtually achieved in The West Indies, is one important aspect of West Indian advance. To be sure, economic opportunity does not automatically follow self-government. The widespread recognition that such development is necessary is, however, a prerequisite to the formulation of the means. In The West Indies, perhaps more than elsewhere in the New World, the modes of living of the present are deeply rooted in the past, and history has a heavy hand.

The islands of the federation are not now places of great opportunity. After three centuries of colonial rule in the British West Indies, Jamaica during the troubled 1930s was described by candid Englishmen as "an imperial slum," and the West Indies as a whole as "the dung heap of the empire." The reasons for such epithets were all too apparent. Political and social change has been painfully slow to develop in the West Indies. Slavery and a plantation economy were at the core of the social and economic life of the colonial British West Indies during the seventeenth and eighteenth centuries. Neither of these institutions really ended when emancipation took place in 1834. The past lives on not only in the many durable ruins that dot West Indian island landscapes, such as the mansions of the planter aristocracy, the stone windmills that were used as early as 1650 to grind sugar cane, and the sugar works in estate yards, but also in West Indian ways of life and thought. The terms "slavery" and "plantation" are closely associated in the West Indies, and both terms call to mind striking contrasts: the great halls of the planters and the miserable huts of the slaves, the indulgence in conspicuous spending and the bondage of an oppressed people, education and interest abroad with exploitation and limited opportunity in the islands; but above all, a concentrated interest in sugar cane. Twentieth-century values, or the wisdom of hindsight, are not being used here to deplore seventeenth-, eighteenth-, and nineteenth-century development and activity in the Caribbean. The twentieth century has enough violence and social injustice of its own. A troubled imperial conscience may be justified on the grounds of present conditions in these islands, without reference to the past.

As many visitors have noted, a study of the West Indies is necessarily a study of poverty. For this there is no easy solution in terms of economic development. In the words of Dr. Eric Williams, written long before his own entry into the political arena, "the observer of whatever kind, and whether he remains in the West Indies for a few weeks or for some years, will find no panacea for the troubles of the colonies. . . . Any conclusions that can be drawn would be in the nature of well-established truisms." [1]

[1] *The Negro in the Caribbean* (Washington, 1942), p. 31.

Many of the recommendations and hopeful comments of recent traveling experts and advisers have been heard time and again. For example, in 1880 one official claimed with respect to the Leeward Islands that "a good deal might be made of the fishery production of these seas if a sufficient attention were devoted to them by people of capital," [2] and many people agreed with him. Enthusiasm for the development of the fishery has been revived from time to time, but the thought has never been translated into action. With few exceptions, poor fishermen with poor gear continue to make a poor living from the sea. The original recommendation, the passing interest, and the lack of action are typical of the West Indies of the past, and go far to explain the present situation.

The West Indies at the time of federation resembles in some ways the Canada of 1867. Some three million West Indians in ten different colonies are making a country out of a group of islands flung across more than a thousand miles of sea. In 1867 some three million people in the four provinces of Nova Scotia, New Brunswick, Quebec, and Ontario began a federation. The logical but by no means inevitable growth of The West Indies involves the entry of British Honduras and British Guiana, to form a federation anchored in the mainlands of Central and South America. Logically or otherwise, within six years Canada had spread across the continent, to become anchored in the east by Prince Edward Island, and in the west by British Columbia. The people of both federations are, or were, agricultural in their way of life and sectional in outlook, and were brought together in federation by political leadership and parliamentary action, not by armed revolt. Both of the

[2] T. B. H. Berkeley, "The Leeward Islands; Their Past and Present Conditions," *Proceedings of the Royal Colonial Institute*, XII (1880–81), 9–50.

languages of Canada are spoken in The West Indies. Similarities between the two federations are not limited to the geographical facts of population, size, isolation, and so on. For both countries, federation was seen as a road to the attainment of some measure of economic self-sufficiency. Canadian success has come about over the course of a century. But in The West Indies economic development must come rapidly to be effective. The federation simply does not have as long a time at its disposal. The following geographical and historical summary may help to explain why.

II

Physical diversity is a marked characteristic of The West Indies. Physiographically, Jamaica is an extension of Central America; along with Cuba, Hispaniola (Haiti and The Dominican Republic), and Puerto Rico, it is part of the Greater Antilles. Trinidad and Tobago are extensions of the Andean mountain system of South America. By contrast, St. Kitts, Nevis, Montserrat, Dominica, St. Lucia, St. Vincent, and Grenada are true oceanic islands, formed by volcanic eruption along a submarine ridge flanking the Caribbean Sea on the east. Anguilla, Barbuda, and Antigua lie along an outer arc composed of old volcanoes that have been eroded, submerged, and capped by marine sediments. Barbados is composed entirely of sediments of continental and marine origin. These differences in geological structure are revealed in the natural landscapes of The West Indies. The gently rolling surface of coralline Barbados contrasts sharply with the towering volcanic piles of the Lesser Antilles, and with the rough mountain country of Jamaica.

Striking differences in climate and vegetation are to be found within the individual islands. The volcanic summits receive from 100 to 300 inches of rain annually, and support luxuriant rain forests, tree ferns, and palm brakes. The upper limits of the forests are generally cloud-capped, sodden with moisture, and bedecked with epiphytes. Within a few miles of these forests there are coastal areas which receive less than 50 inches of rain, where cacti, thorn-scrub, and other drought-resistant vegetation gain local dominance. Temperature is more uniform than rainfall. Winter never comes, and the July average of 80°F differs little from January's 77°F. Even the extreme maximum temperatures are not too uncomfortable in the oceanic islands, swept for the most part by persistent trade winds. The highest annual temperatures recorded on St. Kitts over the past thirty years average 89.9°F, and the lowest 65.5°F.

Natural beauty is to be found almost everywhere on these islands of the Caribbean. Lafcadio Hearn's description of a mountain road on Martinique, written a century ago, is faithful in detail to much of the West Indian landscape today:

All these highways pass through landscapes of amazing beauty— visions of mountains so many tinted and so singular of outline that they would almost seem to have been created for the express purpose of compelling astonishment. This tropic nature appears to call into being nothing ordinary; the shapes which she evokes are always either gracious or odd—and her eccentricities, her extravagances, have a phantastic charm, a grotesqueness as of artistic whim. Even where the landscape view is cut off by high woods, the forms of ancient trees—the infinite interwreathing of vine growths all on fire with violence of blossom colour—the columnar solemnity of great palms, the pliant quivering exquisiteness of bamboo, more than atone for the loss of the horizon. Sometimes you approach a slope covered with what at first glance looks precisely like fine green fur; it is a

first growth of young bamboo. Or you see a hillside covered with
huge green feathers, all shelving down and overlapping as in the
tail of some unutterable bird; these are tree ferns. . . . But one
might write for a hundred years of the sights to be seen upon such
a mountain road.[3]

III

Curiosity about the past is often whetted by observation of
the present cultural landscape. Discussion with a peasant reveals certain attitudes toward the soil and preferences for
certain crops. What is the history behind these attitudes and
preferences? Tombstones in old burial places indicate the
presence of Sephardic Jews of Portuguese descent in many of
these islands during the seventeenth century. Why and how
did they come, what was their importance in the early settlements, and why have they left so little obvious trace? The
ruins of forts and military establishments point back to the
days of Rodney and Nelson, and to the wars of the eighteenth
century, when the wealth of the Indies played an important
role in the affairs of European nations. Why did the islands
later decline? The multiracial society of the federation invites
attention to the origin of the many folk who call themselves
West Indians. Questions like these call for a brief historical
survey of The West Indies.

During the sixteenth century, Drake and Hawkins roamed
the Caribbean under royal patronage. They were followed by
the freebooters and buccaneers of the seventeenth century,
men like Captain Henry Morgan, a pirate turned governor,
and William Dampier, a buccaneer turned naturalist and
writer. Today, Captain Morgan decorates a rum bottle, which
in a way is appropriate enough. Dampier decorates the library

[3] *Two Years in the French West Indies* (New York, 1923), pp. 107–8.

shelf, where he has left fascinating records. Less colorful than these famous freebooters were the settlers who flooded into the British West Indies during the seventeenth century, to establish agricultural colonies that have survived to the present. By a curious coincidence, England and France both established their first successful tropical colony on the same island and in the same year: St. Christopher of the Leewards in 1623. Settlement soon spread to other islands in the Lesser Antilles, and extended to Jamaica in 1655. Within forty years, the aboriginal Indians had been all but eliminated, sugar cane had become the chief crop, and plantations and slavery were firmly established. The wealth of the Indies began to flow to Europe.

The eighteenth century was the economic heyday of the West Indies. It was only after serious consideration that England took Canada as a prize of war in 1763, rather than the rich sugar island of Guadeloupe, 619 square miles in area. (Interestingly enough, a strong argument for choosing Canada was advanced by the British West Indian planters, who wanted to avoid having to compete with Guadeloupe in the home market for sugar.) The nineteenth century saw the decline of British West Indian fortunes, which was not solely the result of the abolition of the slave trade in 1807 and emancipation in 1834–38. The twentieth century has brought some measure of economic prosperity, and marked changes in the political structure of the colonies, culminating in the new federation of 1958.

IV

The Caribbean today is noted as a region of contrasts. English Jamaica, French Haiti, Spanish Puerto Rico are quite similar as to physical environment, remarkably unlike in culture. But even within the federation of The West Indies there is great cultural diversity. Englishmen, Sephardic Jews, Africans, Portuguese, East Indians, Chinese, Syrians, and other peoples have contributed to island populations and ways of life.

Many of the white folk, who established the West Indian economy and whose descendants dominated it for centuries, arrived during the first fifty years of settlement. The identity of these English settlers is revealed in the sailing lists of vessels bound for the Indies in the seventeenth century. The names of many of them have survived as family or estate names in The West Indies down to the present day. (One is often struck by the paucity of family names on the smaller islands. Following emancipation, the Negroes often adopted the names of their former owners as family names. Few names continue to serve many people.) The early white settlers do not appear to have been chiefly husbandmen in the homeland, but rather practitioners of diverse trades, such as "glover, blacksmith, seafaring man, saylemaker, shoemaker, feltmaker, weaver, or tayler." [4] Love of adventure rather than love of the soil characterized the majority.

Most of these folk came from southern England. The counties of Cornwall, Somerset, and particularly Devonshire in the southwest, and also Suffolk, Essex, Hertford, and Oxfordshire bulk large in the early sailing lists. Many failed or emigrated. A few gained great wealth and status. Over the centuries, the white folk of English origin have maintained close ties with the mother country. This passionate attachment

---

[4] John Camden Hotten, *The Original Sailing Lists of Persons of Quality* . . . , *1600–1700* (New York, 1931), p. 151.

to England has been continuously evident in matters of education. And England is seemingly the only place in which to spend a holiday or a long leave, whether one is an expatriate Englishman or a tenth-generation West Indian.

Among the early English settlers tobacco proved to be a profitable crop for the first fifteen years. But by 1640 the quality tobacco grown in Virginia had captured the home market, and the West Indian colonists turned to substitute crops, chiefly cotton, ginger, and indigo. Sugar cane had been grown in the New World since early in the sixteenth century. But it was not produced in the British West Indies during the first few decades, because the technology of sugar manufacture was unknown to the English settlers.

There is some evidence that the technology of sugar making and some of the capital necessary to establish the industry were brought into the British West Indies by Portuguese Jews. Their wealth and business ability had increased sugar production in the early part of the seventeenth century in the northern provinces of Brazil, then under Dutch control. But in 1644 these Sephardic Jews, unwelcome in Brazil because of their refusal to become "new Christians," began to move north. They were a significant part of the population of many West Indian islands between 1650 and 1725, but then withdrew, except for small communities in Barbados and Jamaica. During the period 1690 to 1710 they were reported to have made up 25 percent of the merchant class of Charlestown in Nevis.

Once the knowledge of how to manufacture sugar was acquired, sugar cane spread rapidly through the islands. Its survival as the chief agricultural crop of the federation 300 years later is some indication of its suitability to the climatic

and edaphic conditions of the area. According to Richard
Ligon, the English on Barbados were experimenting with
sugar in 1647; by 1650 they were producing it successfully.
Ten years later sugar cane was the principal crop in all the
French and English colonies of the Lesser Antilles. The establishment of sugar cane was of paramount importance for the
future of the colonies. It disrupted the pattern of settlement
within the islands; it forced a considerable proportion of the
white small landholders to emigrate; over the centuries it has
produced, on the one hand, great wealth, and on the other,
social problems that seem to defy solution.

Sugar gave rise to a planter class in the British West Indies.
Tobacco, cotton, and ginger had been raised on plots of a
few acres, but the growth of sugar cane and the manufacture
of muscovado, or unrefined sugar, required large acreage and
much capital. Mid-seventeenth-century maps of the Leeward
Islands and Barbados show closely located settlements of small
farmers. With the transition to sugar, successful farmers bought
out their less successful neighbors, and the numerous small
farms were amalgamated into larger estates. Displaced whites
in the Lesser Antilles moved on to less crowded islands, such as
Jamaica, and to North America. The last half of the seventeenth
century was a period of rapid agricultural development in the
British West Indies. Sugar plantations and slavery became
firmly established, wealth was produced, and a planter aristocracy emerged.

Throughout the seventeenth century the clearing of land
for agriculture proceeded apace. The reports of early travelers
indicate that coastal areas were rapidly cleared of their forest
cover. Large acreages in sugar cane made for a tidy, almost
European, countryside. But the amenities of life were at first

difficult to attain in the islands. Estate and town buildings were rude huts, "of ordinary timber, covered with thatch, very few shingled," according to one colonial governor.[5] The towns were busy places; there were perhaps more merchants in the English colonies during the seventeenth century than later, when the planters got into the habit of buying their provisions directly from American vessels, and ordering the rest of their supplies from London and Bristol. Christopher Jeaffreson, a young squire and a keen man of business in the colonies, summed up one aspect of the situation in a letter to his associate in London:

As for your chaires that do not fold, your bedticks, your striped curtains and vallances, your carpets of low prices, too many of these things will soon cloy the country, because they are not but for the better sort. The most part here lye in hammakers, sit upon benches, cloath themselves in rough cloth, and never cover the table but at meals.[6]

Not until later did the West Indian planter gain his reputation for high living, and aspire to a life in England supported by a flow of wealth from an island estate.

The link between sugar and Negro slavery is very close. Negroes were present in the West Indies as early as 1635, but the demand for them increased manyfold after sugar cane, with its great need for field labor, became the chief crop. The business of introducing Negro slaves really got underway in 1670, when the Royal African Company was formed. Nevis became the slave market for the Royal African Company in the Leewards. The Negroes were landed, washed, oiled,

[5] Colonel William Stapleton, Governor of the Leeward Islands in 1676. See Calendar of State Papers, Colonial Series, America and West Indies, 1675–1676, No. 1152, 22 Nov. 1676.

[6] *Christopher Jeaffreson, A Young Squire of the Seventeenth Century (from the Papers of Christopher Jeaffreson)* (London, 1878), p. 190.

marched through town behind a drummer, and sold in the town square. The eighteenth-century historian, Bryan Edwards, estimates that more than 600,000 Africans were introduced as slaves into Jamaica alone between 1700 and 1786. Although the institution of slavery was abolished in 1834, many of its effects linger on. Not the least of these is the unwillingness of the Negro to associate himself with a preslavery past in Africa.

The Negro predominates by a wide margin in all The West Indies save Trinidad, and white folk are everywhere a small minority: 5 percent in Barbados, 3 percent in St. Vincent and Trinidad, 2 percent or less elsewhere. But West Indian life is basically European, not African, in matters of culture. Negroes in The West Indies neither recognize nor exhibit societal ties stemming from Old World origins. Intermingling and common patterns of life over the past three centuries have eliminated tribal and other differences which in the beginning appear to have been strong. In the days of the slave trade, Africans were identified by tribe or region as Corromantes, Ibboes, Whydahs, and Congo and Angola Negroes. In the Leeward Islands the West African Negroes known as Corromantes were held in high esteem as slaves, and were noted for their spirit and bravery. In contrast, the Ibboes were considered timid and prone to suicide, a tendency not overlooked by the prospective buyer. The Whydahs, or Papaws, as they were known in the West Indies, were thought more tractable, although addicted to gambling. According to Bryan Edwards, the Congo and Angola natives were more fit for domestic service than for field labor. On the whole, however, most planters assigned their slaves to heavy or light tasks on the basis of age and sex. Tribal differences among the slaves are little mentioned in West Indian literature, and appear to have had but slight influence upon life in the West Indies. Owing to the conditions of New World slavery, the African past was rapidly forgotten.

Two centuries of slavery have, to a considerable extent, cut off British West Indian Negroes from their African heritage. Whatever this heritage may have contributed elsewhere, in these islands it is in small evidence save for certain aspects of religion and music.

The eighteenth century in the Caribbean was marked by war, but also by prosperity. West Indian planters became familiar figures in London, rich absentee landlords more active in conspicuous consumption than in primary production. In the West Indies, however, town life was in a state of decline. As there were few middlemen in trade, social and economic life centered on the plantations. Each was a little world in itself, a farm for the raising of sugar cane and a factory for the production of sugar. Substantial buildings were erected in the plantation yards for the grinding of cane and the boiling of sugar. But the average plantation was not large. In the Lesser Antilles most plantations had less than one hundred acres in sugar cane, and fewer than one hundred and fifty slaves. Estates with more than two hundred Negroes were exceptional.

Slaves were allowed to raise ground provisions such as yams and sweet potatoes on land not devoted to sugar cane. On many plantations they were given Saturday afternoons off to work on these garden plots. The production of foodstuffs did not meet the demand, and the islands soon became dependent upon North American sources of food, such as salt cod, flour, and corn. Since the export of sugar and molasses required staves and hoops, an important trade in timber was established with the North American colonies.

Slave deaths always outnumbered births, so that planters had to depend upon the slave trade to keep their labor force. The canny John Pinney, a planter in the Leeward Islands in the late eighteenth century, encouraged childbearing among his slave force by gifts of baby linen on appropriate occasions, but without conspicuous success.

The humanitarian zeal that was to bring about such diverse results as prison reform and poor relief, as well as abolition of the slave trade and, later, emancipation, appeared early in the British West Indies. In 1671 the Quakers urged their converts on Barbados to treat slaves mildly, and to grant them liberty after some years of servitude. This free advice was not translated immediately into costly action, but it is significant that the awakening interest in the welfare of the slaves came from groups outside the established church. The Moravian Brethren founded missions in the British West Indies about the middle of the eighteenth century, as did other religious sects. Not until 1794 did the Anglican Church begin missionary work in the Caribbean colonies.

The abolition of the slave trade in 1807, and emancipation three decades later, crowned the efforts of humanitarians in England and the West Indies.

These reforms were accompanied and followed by a period of sharp economic decline. For this, however, emancipation of the slaves was neither the sole nor the chief cause. Powerful economic forces operated to the disadvantage of the British West Indian sugar islands. Sugar production was being extended to foreign areas like Cuba and Brazil, where the soil was rich and the labor supply relatively ample. The drift to free trade brought a decrease and finally an end to preferential treatment in the home market, and the British West Indies could not compete on an equal basis with more efficient producers. But if emancipation was only one of many causes of economic decline, it had other far-reaching consequences in the colonies.

For one thing, it brought into being a class of small farmers. Along with his freedom, the Negro gained the right to refuse to work (a more basic freedom than the right to work). On the larger islands, notably on Jamaica, the availability of land for squatting enabled him to withdraw from the labor market, and to engage in something approaching subsistence agriculture. The rough mountain land of interior Jamaica looked better to him than the canefield and the hut in the estate yard. The new small farmers came to be called "peasants," but they lacked the common characteristics of peasants elsewhere, such as respect for their own ways, love of the soil, and a long association with place. The dignity of agricultural life is still absent in The West Indies, a striking and important fact in a country with a land-hungry population. To many West Indians the term "peasant" generally connotes a farmer of low status.

Few economic plants entered Caribbean agriculture along with the Negro. The greater yam, *Dioscorea alata,* was introduced into the New World probably more because of European recognition of its value as a slave food than because of Negro interest in it. The well-documented introduction in the late eighteenth century of the breadfruit, *Artocarpus communis,* was another case of European interest. The crops and the agricultural techniques of the small Negro farmers bespeak recent rather than ancient associations, are more closely related to New World than to African experience and techniques, and are for the most part crude and unsatisfactory. The commercial agriculture practiced by Englishmen in the tropics provided no useful lessons to small farmers oriented toward subsistence or the local market. The absence of capital, of equipment, of transport facilities, and of agricultural education in any local context has further retarded them. The land settlement programs popular at present recognize but seldom solve the problem. A peasantry is not easily created.

Emancipation was followed by a labor shortage in the British West Indies, most severely felt in Jamaica and Trinidad. On the smaller islands, where most of the land was already in private ownership, the Negro had little opportunity to acquire a freehold. A series of restrictive laws limited his opportunities to seek work elsewhere, and he usually remained within walking distance of the old plantation, on which he became a day laborer at a wage of about one shilling a day. Economic bonds replaced the legal bonds of slavery; emancipation from these did not come until more than a century later.

Legal emancipation, however, brought the poor of many other lands into the West Indies; the multiracial society of today is the direct result. The labor shortage was met by the introduction of workers, in order of increasing numbers, from England, Africa, Madeira, Hong Kong, and India. Immigration still continues, though on a greatly reduced scale; Chinese and Syrians have arrived up to the mid-twentieth century. Up to 1917 East Indians continued to enter on contract, subject to a system of indenture. The ability of West Indians to recognize the right of minorities to be different and to practice their own ways is worthy of recognition and emulation.

Port of Spain, Trinidad, for instance, is Spanish and French in background, English by adoption, and shows racial and cultural traces of Africa, India, Pakistan, China, and the Levant.

Nineteenth-century immigration failed, however, to stem West Indian economic decline. Observer after observer recounted the familiar story: abandonment of land and estate houses, tumbling values of property, poor husbandry, and little effort or ability to keep up with technological changes in the manufacture of sugar. The tree fern, *Cyathea arborea,* is a dependable indicator today of areas where agriculture has recently been abandoned. Accounts between 1850 and 1900 record the widespread occurrence of the tree fern in many islands. As land value dropped, tenant farming increased; dwindling profits were earned at the expense of soil exhaustion and erosion. In 1897 a West India Royal Commission recommended the diversification of agriculture and the modernization of the sugar industry. Some effort was put into carrying out both proposals, with modest success, but forty years later a new royal commission found conditions as bad as before.

v

The history of Old World settlement in the British Caribbean yields no evidence from which one can forecast an easy future for the new federation. Political and social reform, long in abeyance, has accelerated in recent decades. But political independence is meaningless without economic independence, and the limited resources of the federation, coupled with the history of their use, give rise to apprehension about the future.

The evil effects of three centuries of settlement in these

islands are easily to be seen. Soil erosion is a particularly serious result of the economic decline of the nineteenth century. Low financial returns from land, chronic in the West Indies for 150 years, are an open invitation to exploitative practices. The rehabilitation of soil-stripped slopes is costly but necessary, and is now in process on islands from Jamaica to Barbados. Such good land as exists has for the most part been in use since the seventeenth century. There is virtually nowhere else in the islands for agriculture to expand, and the land frontiers in British Guiana and British Honduras are presently unavailable, technologically as well as politically.

Present improvements over the recent past may justify some optimism, but the limitations of available resources make the future of The West Indies uncertain. No member of the federation is rich enough to be able to give much more than it receives; all of the islands live too close to poverty to indulge in the luxury of philanthropy. Financial responsibilities must be portioned out with care, because the difference between what each member of the federation must do and what it can do is negligible. The West Indians cannot afford to be anything other than economic realists.

The Political Development

of The West Indies

DOUGLAS G. ANGLIN

The political institutions of The West Indies are among the
newest and the oldest in the world. Although the first federal
parliament was formally opened only in April, 1958, the be-
ginnings of constitutional government in the territories go
back more than three hundred years. This element of con-
tinuity in West Indian political experience is one significant
factor distinguishing The West Indies from many other countries, principally in Asia and Africa, which are also emerging
from colonial status at the present time.

The first representative assembly in the Caribbean, and one
of the earliest anywhere in the Americas, was held in Barbados
in 1639, just twenty years after Virginia's House of Burgesses
convened. Subsequently the Old Representative System, as it
came to be called, was extended to most of the other British
colonies acquired prior to the American Revolution. Under
this form of government there was a governor responsible to
London but to some extent dependent, particularly in matters of finance, upon a locally elected—and often uncoopera-
tive—House of Assembly. The result was constant conflict
and frequent deadlock. In Jamaica, for example, in 1755

the governor felt compelled to dissolve a recalcitrant assembly three times within a period of three months. On the mainland similar incessant strife led to American independence and to responsible cabinet government in Canada. But neither of these alternatives was open to the West Indies.

The constitutional crisis there came to a head in the middle decades of the nineteenth century, following the emancipation of the slaves and the loss, after 1846, of the virtual monopoly which West Indian sugar had held in the British market. Socially, these changes transformed West Indian ways of life; economically, their consequences were calamitous; politically, they exacerbated relations between executive and legislature. Effective control of local legislatures remained firmly in the hands of white oligarchs, who were not disposed to relinquish it to the Negro majorities.

This political system had been tenable as long as most of the Negroes were classified as chattels, but once they were accorded the status of citizens, the denial of equal political rights became increasingly difficult to justify. Yet the bulk of the population was fitted neither by education nor by experience to assume any significant role in government. Nor did responsible government on the Canadian model offer a solution, for it assumed the existence of a representative assembly. In the West Indies, this was out of the question. The only way to assure civil order and to protect the interests of both majority and minority was, in fact, to give up self-government.

The logic of this position had long been apparent, but it took a serious revolt among Negro laborers in Jamaica in 1865 to reveal the extent to which self-government had degenerated into misgovernment. The following year the Old Representative System there was swept aside and replaced by crown colony government. This system had already been introduced into the colonies acquired during the Napoleonic Wars, notably Trinidad. By the end of the nineteenth century it had become general throughout the West Indies, except in Barbados and the Bahamas, where the Old Representative System survived virtually intact until after the Second World War.

In the other islands the elected assemblies responsible to local electorates gave way to appointed legislative councils composed of crown nominees. As creatures of the executive, they had relatively little power. Paradoxically, however, the new nominated legislative councils were in practice more representative than the supposedly representative assemblies they replaced.

Constitutional regression could not, of course, be accepted as permanent. Indeed, as early as 1884 an elective element was restored in the Jamaican legislature, though the governor retained an official majority. Forty years later, with the upsurge of nationalism following the First World War, a similar step was taken in Trinidad and, subsequently, in the other West Indian territories. None of these reforms, however, altered the basic structure of the crown colony system, which lasted up to and, in some cases, even beyond the Second World War. Although this lengthy period of imperial trusteeship generated considerable local discontent, it did serve two purposes. It carried the West Indies through a critical period when premature constitutional reform might have meant restoration of power to the European minority, with results similar to those in East, Central, and South Africa today. It also permitted an experienced administrative structure to develop in advance of the transfer of political power.

In contrast to the leisurely pace of the past, West Indian constitutional innovation since the Second World War, though less precipitate than in many other parts of the world, has been rapid. Several factors account for this accelerated evolution. The aggravation of West Indian poverty during the prolonged depression of the interwar years engendered a sense of acute injustice, which flared up in the labor riots of the late 1930s. Economic distress turned men's minds to political action; political parties emerged to spearhead demands for reform. And the war generated new pressures for far-reaching political and economic change.

The principal stages of constitutional reform were the restoration of representative government, the adoption of a democratic franchise, and the introduction of ministerial responsibility. Jamaica again led the way. In 1944, after sixty years of constitutional stagnation, the Jamaicans gained universal adult suffrage and a wholly elected assembly. Other reforms have followed, and complete internal self-government was attained in July, 1959. The governor no longer has the power of veto, and only vestigial powers of reservation and disallowance remain. Trinidad, too, has made rapid strides toward self-government, and will soon be abreast of Jamaica. Barbados, where a cabinet system was instituted at the beginning of 1958, is not far behind. Even the smaller territories have achieved a substantial measure of self-government. Their demand for equality is no more than natural, though the wisdom of permitting a proliferation of petty parliaments and cabinets may be doubted. Complete independence for any of the island units individually, save perhaps Jamaica, is not contemplated. As British spokesmen have emphasized, it is "clearly impossible in the modern world for the present separate communities [in the West Indies], small and isolated as most of them are, to achieve and maintain full self-government on their own." [1] The implications of this pointed comment were not lost on West Indian political leaders; the price of independence was federation.

II

Although federation of the British West Indies did not become a practical possibility until after the Second World War, some form of closer association has long been considered desirable. During the interwar period a number of official British missions visited the Caribbean to explore the problem on the spot. The future Lord Halifax, sent in 1921–22, was impressed with the advantages of greater unity, but he was convinced that the parochialism of the islanders rendered "anything approaching a general federal system" both "inopportune and impracticable." The West India Royal Commission of 1939 likewise doubted "whether the time [was] yet ripe for the introduction of any large measure of federation," but noted that "local opinion [had] made a considerable advance in the direction of political unity" in the intervening years.

Meanwhile, a number of common intergovernmental services had been built up and jointly financed, though often in the teeth of fierce local opposition. In 1919 a West Indies Court of Appeal was created; in 1924 the Imperial College of Tropical Agriculture was founded in Trinidad; and in 1934 a West Indian trade commissioner was appointed to Canada. In order

[1] *Closer Association of the British West Indian Colonies,* Command Paper No. 7120 (London, H.M. Stationery Office, 1947), p. 9.

further to "overcome local prejudice against federation" and to pave the way towards eventual political union, the Royal Commission advocated "amalgamation" of the Leewards and Windwards and the unification, so far as possible, of all West Indian public services.

One of the most important results of the Royal Commission Report was the appointment in 1940 of a comptroller for development and welfare in the West Indies, to advise on plans to raise living standards in the area and on the distribution of the colonial development and welfare funds recently voted by the British Parliament. Together with a number of wartime agencies of cooperation, the Development and Welfare Organization contributed substantially to the administrative integration of the territories. At the same time, political consciousness among the masses continued to grow. For their leaders, the demand for self-government came to be associated increasingly with the realization of a federation. Pressure for political freedom and social justice, rather than considerations of administrative convenience or economy, now provided the main impetus to closer union.

A further factor was the revolution in inter-island communications brought about by the advent of the airplane. Before the war, direct steamship service between the territories—where it existed at all—was slow and infrequent. Lord Halifax reported in 1922 that "the postal authorities in Jamaica [were] usually compelled to send mails for Trinidad, Barbados and British Guiana *via* either England, New York or Halifax"; this sometimes took weeks or even months. Since the Second World War the situation has changed radically. As one report pointed out in 1950, "now it is far less troublesome and time-consuming to assemble a fully representative gathering in this region than it was in 1787 in North America or even a meeting of the British Parliament before the advent of railways." [2]

The dramatic change in the West Indian political climate—clearly apparent at the West Indian Conference in Barbados in March, 1944—persuaded the British government that the time had come to press for early action on federation. In March, 1945, the secretary of state for the colonies announced British support for "the establishment of [a] federation at the appropriate time," and called upon the colonial legislatures to voice their views. All but the Bahamas responded favorably. Thereupon Arthur Creech-Jones, the new colonial secretary, convened a conference at Montego Bay, Jamaica, in September, 1947, "to consider the formulation of proposals for closer association" of the West Indies.

The Montego Bay Conference accepted the principle of federation, on condition that the association be a loose one. Although considerable opposition was voiced, a compromise federal resolution gained the support of every delegation except the Guianese. The task of framing a federal constitution was delegated to a Standing Closer Association Committee, composed of West Indians chosen by local legislatures.

This committee's recommendations—approved in principle by all the colonial legislatures except those of British Guiana and British Honduras—were reviewed at a conference in London in April, 1953. Out of this emerged a revised plan for a British Caribbean Federation, subsequently endorsed by the separate territories. The issues still outstanding were settled, with some gentle prodding by the Colonial Office, at a con-

[2] *Report of the British Caribbean Standing Closer Association Committee, 1948–49,* Col[onial] No. 255 (London, H.M. Stationery Office, 1950), p. 16.

ference convened in London in 1956, following which parliament passed the British Caribbean Federation Act. February 23rd, the date on which the 1956 conference report was signed, is celebrated in The West Indies as Federation Day.

Meanwhile, preparatory steps were being taken to bring the federation into operation. A Regional Economic Committee to advise on both inter- and extraterritorial economic relations was appointed in 1951. For years the R.E.C. was the only meeting place for interterritorial ministerial consultation. In 1955 Sir Stephen Luke, comptroller for development and welfare in the West Indies, was designated commissioner for the preparation of the federal organization, and experts were appointed to prepare reports on the fiscal, civil service, and judicial implications of federation. A year later the delegates to the 1956 London conference created a Standing Federation Committee. This prefederal executive quickly plunged into the task of organizing departments of government, appointing key officials, and procuring temporary accommodation, drawing up interim legislation and regulations, and attending to all the other problems, large and small, associated with the establishment of a modern state.

The issue which aroused most controversy was the choice of the federal capital.[3] The Standing Closer Association Committee in 1950 had proposed that the seat of government should be in Trinidad, but this suggestion was opposed by Jamaica and Barbados. In 1953 Grenada was tentatively selected, but this too evoked a storm of protest. One newspaper objected to the choice of an "island which must be approached in a punt and where the drinking water for the federal legis-

[3] See David Lowenthal, "The West Indies Chooses a Capital," *The Geographical Review*, XLVIII (1958), 336–64.

lators must be carried in barrels." It was doubtful whether any of the smaller islands could meet the requirements of a national capital. The London conference of 1956 referred the issue to a federal capital commission, composed of three British experts. The commission ruled out the smaller islands and recommended Barbados, Jamaica, and Trinidad in that order. Trinidad came last on the list because of "the instability of that island's politics and the low standard accepted in its public life." That settled the matter; provoked by this "insult," the standing federation committee promptly chose Trinidad as the capital site.

The preliminaries were completed in the early months of 1958. In January the Constitution came into force. Lord Hailes, a Conservative peer and former cabinet minister, assumed office as first governor-general. In March and April the first federal elections took place, Sir Grantley Adams of Barbados was chosen prime minister, a cabinet and senate were appointed, and parliament was opened amid royal splendor. Federation became a reality; The West Indies was born.

III

The West Indies does not embrace all the British territories in and around the Caribbean. From the first, the Bahamas took no interest in the proposed federation. The British Virgin Islands, too, preferred to retain close economic ties with American Caribbean territories rather than to join the new federation. Whatever interest the British Virgin Islands may have had in federation was lost when the Standing Closer Association Committee denied her a seat in the Senate. The other territories felt that, with less than half the population of tiny

Montserrat, the Virgin Islands was too small to merit separate representation. Unless her tourist industry becomes a substantial dollar earner, it is hardly likely that she would be welcomed into the federation other than as a non-voting semi-dependency like the Cayman Islands and Turks and Caicos Islands.

The two mainland territories, British Guiana and British Honduras, have likewise rejected federation. But their decision may not be final. Both territories participated in the Montego Bay Conference of 1947, the Standing Closer Association Committee, and the Regional Economic Committee. They continue to send observers to certain federal meetings.

"British Honduras," declared the federal prime minister, "has no more intention of joining the Federation than I have of going aloft in a Sputnik." [4] Anti-federation sentiment in British Honduras stems partly from the fact that Jamaica, her nearest British neighbor, lies more than 700 miles to the east. Although many Hondurans are the descendants of Jamaicans, the mainlanders generally fear Jamaican aggression and are unhappy about the prospect of immigration from the overcrowded West Indies into comparatively empty British Honduras. Moreover, British Honduran currency is tied to the American dollar, rather than to sterling. Finally, certain leaders of the dominant People's United Party have, at least until recently, sought to wring political and economic concessions from the British by flirting with Guatemala, which claims sovereignty over Belize.

British Guiana has also felt a sense of continental destiny.

[4] *The Parliamentary Debates, Official Report, Proceedings and Debates of the First Session (1958) of the First House of Representatives of The West Indies, Constituted under The West Indies (Federation) Order-in-Council, 1957,* 7th Sitting, Monday, 16th June, 1958, col. 462.

She alone refused to accept the principle of federation at Montego Bay in 1947, and her Legislative Council rejected the report of the Standing Closer Association Committee. With ten times the area of the whole federation and a rich though undeveloped interior, British Guiana is anxious not to become a dumping ground for the overflow population of the islands. On the other hand, she is keenly interested in a West Indian customs union, particularly as a means of marketing her rice; if she cannot obtain the benefits of customs union without federation, she may feel compelled to accept it.

The decisive considerations, however, are likely to be ethnic and political. The predominantly Negro opposition party, the People's National Congress, which is affiliated with Adams's Federal Labour Party, favors federation, but Dr. Cheddi Jagan's governing People's Progressive Party, dominantly East Indian, opposes it. Dr. Jagan and his party are more concerned with achieving internal self-government for British Guiana than with federation with The West Indies, even an independent West Indies, and intend to postpone the decision until Guianese independence has been realized. There is little to indicate that they would even then favor federation. But British Guiana does attend sessions of the Regional Council of Ministers, participate in the West Indies Currency Board, contribute her share towards support of the University College of The West Indies, and permit appeals from her own courts to the Federal Supreme Court.

Should any of these British territories opt for federation, they could be admitted by an order-in-council passed in London. In contrast, if any non-British Caribbean territory should want to join, the consent of each of the ten territorial legislatures would be required. There is no reason to believe that this would be any easier to obtain in The West Indies than it would be in other federal states. For this reason, if for no other, the idea of a gradual extension of The West Indies to embrace the other islands of the Caribbean is somewhat implausible.

Concern over the disparity in size and resources of units within the federation was one consideration which prompted the British to urge federation of the Leewards and Windwards. Not only was the scheme rejected by the territories concerned, but the eighty-five-year-old federation of the Leeward Islands was dissolved in 1956. Thus the seven separate colonies, all with populations under 100,000, were admitted as unit members of the federation along with Jamaica, Trinidad and Tobago, and Barbados.

IV

Political parties in The West Indies are little more than twenty years old. Like the trade unions, with which most of them are closely connected, they first emerged during the late 1930s. Progress towards stable party structures has varied, however. Outside of Jamaica and Barbados, parties have until recently been little more than shifting alliances centering around individuals. The charismatic politician is still significant, but more permanent patterns of political alignments are now emerging.

Not until 1956, with the formation of Dr. Eric Williams's People's National Movement, did Trinidad first experience real party politics. Unfortunately, party lines there have to a disquieting degree split along racial lines. The People's National Movement is widely regarded as the Negro party and the opposition Democratic Labour Party as the Indian party. Although this development is universally deplored, each side accuses the other of having deliberately exploited racial tensions for political advantage.

The Jamaica party system has had the greatest impact on the shaping of national political parties because it is the oldest and best organized and its leaders are the most experienced. The present governing party is the People's National Party, founded by Norman Manley in 1938. The more conservative Jamaica Labour Party is the political arm of the Bustamente Industrial Trade Union. Its president is Manley's cousin and inveterate political foe, Sir Alexander Bustamente. These two veterans are not only, respectively, premier and leader of the opposition in Jamaica, but also (until Bustamente's resignation in May, 1960) extra-parliamentary leaders of the two national parties, the Federal Labour Party and the Democratic Labour Party.

The West Indies Federal Labour Party, inaugurated in 1956, is made up of a number of territorial affiliates: Manley's People's National Party in Jamaica, Sir Grantley Adams's Barbados Labour Party, and several labour parties in the smaller islands; Williams's People's National Movement in Trinidad is an ally, but not a full member. With this impressive backing, it was assumed that the Federal Labour Party was assured of a comfortable majority in the March, 1958, elections, if not of a landslide victory. The outcome was something of a shock. The Federal Labour Party won only 22 of the 45 seats in the House of Representatives, while the Democratic Labour Party carried 20 seats, including a majority in both Jamaica and Trinidad. The balance of power was held by an independent from Barbados and two Grenada United Labour

Party members. Although the latter had originally been elected as Federal Labour Party supporters, they promptly declared their votes would be "fluid."

The Democratic Labour Party is a loose collection of territorial parties and individuals formed in 1957 by Bustamente. If the Federal Labour Party stands for independence, federation, and socialism, the Democratic Labour Party, to the extent that it has a policy, tends to be less militant in its nationalism, lukewarm towards federation and, despite the inevitable inclusion of "Labour" in its title, socially more conservative. The Democratic Labour Party has not, however, formulated or pursued any consistent national policy. Many of its leaders, while very able, are highly idiosyncratic men of little formal education who differ sharply on national issues. The rank and file of the party is even more heterogeneous. One reason is that much of its strength comes from ill-assorted minority groups, such as Roman Catholics, East Indians, planters, and representatives of commercial interests, who for quite different reasons feel threatened by the majority.

Internal stresses and strains in the Democratic Labour Party came to a head in January, 1959, when Albert Gomes, a leader in the Trinidad branch, objected to the increasingly anti-federationist tone of the party's Jamaican spokesmen in the federal parliament, and accused Bustamente of sinister machinations. In a blistering reply, Bustamente threatened to resign as leader. "I would sooner associate with scorpions," he declared, "than stay leader of a party which includes Gomes. Jamaica is my first love, not the Federation." Gomes promptly apologized, and the crisis passed, but the episode illustrates the fragility of the opposition party. Were the Democratic Labour Party to disintegrate, the Federal Labour Party too might experience difficulty in maintaining unity. As it is, recurrent public displays of disharmony among top leaders of the Federal Labour Party are dangerously disruptive. Williams, for instance, recently denounced Adams as "a stooge of the Colonial Office," and Adams in turn has accused Williams of making charges which were deliberately "inaccurate, misleading and untruthful."

West Indian political parties are formally patterned on the British model, but are in many respects characteristically American, seeking to be all things to all men. This is perhaps inevitable in a far-flung federation. Certainly the existence of any kind of national parties offers better prospects for the survival of the federation than would purely regional parties.

v

The political institutions of The West Indies are, in the main, almost slavishly patterned on the British parliamentary system.

As The West Indies is not yet independent, the governor-general is appointed by the queen on the advice of the British government, to which he is in some measure responsible. Normally, he is a constitutional head of state. In the exercise of his prerogative of dissolving parliament or dismissing ministers, he is to "act as nearly as may be in accordance with the constitutional conventions that apply . . . in the United Kingdom." [5] But he was clearly meant to be more than a figurehead, particularly during the formative years of the federation. The 1958 constitution contained thirty references specifically empowering the governor-general to act "in his discretion" or "in

[5] *Instructions passed under the Royal Sign Manual and Signet to the Governor General and Commander-in-Chief of The West Indies, 20th August, 1957* (London, H.M. Stationery Office, 1957), section 3.

his individual judgment." Some of these provisions accorded him sweeping political powers, much greater, in fact, than those wielded by the governors of the larger units. Thus, the governor-general personally appointed all the senators, justices of the Federal Supreme Court, and members of the Public Service Commission. In certain circumstances, he could remove any or all of them. He could refuse assent to any bill or reserve it for review by the British government. He could decide any urgent matter, however important, on his own, if time did not permit him to consult his cabinet. He had the discretionary "power to make appointments to offices in the public service of the Federation (including promotions and transfers) and to dismiss and to exercise disciplinary control over officers," and he was not required to accept the advice even of his own Public Service Commission. In actual practice, however, Governor-General Hailes availed himself of few of these special constitutional powers. In August, 1960, he formally relinquished a number of them and was required to respect British practice in the exercise of most of his other personal powers.

Originally the principal instrument of federal policy was the Council of State. This body differed from the usual cabinet in that the governor-general convened, attended, and presided over it. Moreover, three senior civil servants designated by the governor-general had the right to participate in its discussions. A legacy from crown colony government, this arrangement was justified by a belief that the views of responsible officials should be given full weight in the highest council of the nation during the early years of federation. In January, 1960, however, Britain agreed that the Council of State should be abolished in favor of full cabinet government, and this has now been done.

The procedure for appointing the first prime minister was also unusual. As there was a possibility that party lines in parliament might not be clear-cut, with consequent uncertainty concerning the majority leader, the prime minister was first elected by the House of Representatives and only subsequently appointed by the governor-general who, therefore, exercised no discretion whatsoever. However, it is now the responsibility of the governor-general to judge who is "best able to command the confidence of a majority of the members of the House."

The prime minister is free to nominate the ten ministers in his cabinet but, contrary to the usual practice, his choice is limited to those who are *already* members of either federal house. This requirement is unduly restrictive, especially as the Senate and House of Representatives now have only nineteen and forty-five members respectively. Moreover, it mitigates against adequate representation of the various territories, racial groups, religions, class interests, and the two sexes. This restriction, in conjunction with the rule that forbids legislators to occupy federal and territorial positions at the same time, deprives the federal government of the services of many of the most prominent West Indian leaders. Several of these, including the national leaders of the two federal parties, chose to remain in their own bailiwicks. And the defeat of the West Indian Federal Labour Party in Jamaica and Trinidad eliminated other promising candidates of cabinet caliber.

Prime Minister Sir Grantley Adams therefore faced a difficult task when he came to form his first cabinet. He eventually included one woman, but no East Indian for the simple reason that none was elected on the government side of the House. The most distressing feature, however, is the territorial imbalance. The eight smallest units, with less than a quarter of the total population, have eight out of the eleven cabinet seats, including all the key portfolios. In fact, a majority of the positions have gone to four territories with less than a tenth of the population, whereas Jamaica, with over half the federal population, has only two cabinet posts, only one of which carries a portfolio.

The federal legislature consists of the queen, a senate, and a house of representatives. A Caribbean Labour Congress proposal of 1947 called for a single chamber, but the Standing Closer Association Committee decisively favored a bicameral legislature, principally because it seemed an essential prerequisite in a federal state. The Senate, however, has subordinate status. The prime minister must be chosen from the lower house, ensuring that the cabinet shall be responsible to the House of Representatives alone. Money bills cannot be introduced in the Senate. And the Senate may delay the passage of legislation for a maximum of one year in the case of ordinary bills and one month in the case of money bills. Finally, members of the Senate are nominated, as in Canada, rather than elected, as in the United States and Australia. They are appointed for a fixed term of five years, and not for life. However, though subordinate, the Senate is not meant to be unimportant. Two seats in the cabinet are reserved for senators, though at present there are three, none carrying a portfolio.

The federal aspect of the Senate is emphasized in two ways. The first is the method of appointment, in which the national government plays no formal part. The governor-general chooses the senators after consultation with the cabinets of the individual territories. When the first appointments were made, the governor-general agreed to all the nominations of the territorial governments except two—one each in Jamaica and Trinidad. In both of these cases, he appointed instead senators proposed by the opposition parties, which had in fact won a majority of the seats in Trinidad and Jamaica in the federal elections. Even this exercise of the governor-general's personal prerogative was challenged by Manley in Jamaica as an abrogation of the constitution. There was no legal justification for this complaint, but in the course of time the acceptance of territorial majority party nominations is likely to become the normal if not the invariable rule.

The second federal aspect of the Senate is the principle of equal territorial representation. There are two senators from each of the units except Montserrat, which has only one (and this is likely to be rectified shortly). This is a normal device in federal states to balance the preponderant influence which representation by population gives the larger territories in the lower house. But in The West Indies, representation by population was not, at first, the rule in the House of Representatives. As the Standing Closer Association Committee reported:

in fixing numbers, we found it necessary to take into account not numbers only, but such matters as economic development and productivity, financial stability and so on [mostly "so on," it would seem]. . . . The result is that our proposed allocation of seats defies reduction to even the most complicated mathematical formula relating it to population figures.

The distribution finally agreed upon in 1953 gave Jamaica only 38 percent of the seats, considerably less than the 52 percent she would be entitled to on a population basis. Trinidad too was underrepresented, while Barbados and the smaller units were overrepresented to a greater or lesser degree. However, within a year after federation Jamaica threatened to secede unless seats were reallocated on the basis of population, and early in 1960 preliminary agreement was reached among territorial delegates that the new constitution should change the membership of the House of Representatives from 45 to 64 by increasing Jamaica's representation from 17 to 31 (48 percent of the total) and Trinidad's from 10 to 15.

VI

The West Indies is one of the weakest federal systems ever to come into existence. One observer has called it a "ghost federation." This is apparent in the limited legislative authority of the federal government, the failure to agree on a customs union, the restrictions on migration between the islands, and the shaky state of federal finances. As the colonial secretary remarked at the conclusion of the 1956 London conference, in a typically British understatement: "It cannot be said that [the federation's] government powers will at the outset be strong, nor its field of activity large."

This weakness was intended. West Indian leaders had agreed that the main sphere of federal responsibility should be external relations; the negotiation of trade agreements, immigration and emigration, exchange control, defense, overseas representation, and political relations with other countries. The federal government was specifically empowered to implement international agreements even on matters which normally would come within the sole jurisdiction of the territories. The other principal area of central authority is inter-island and international communications: shipping and navigation, civil aviation, postal services, telephones and telegraphs, and radio and television.

Even these limited powers, however, were not to be fully exercised by the federal government at the start. "Only those subjects . . . which [were] essential to the existence of the Federation as such" [6] became its immediate exclusive responsibility. These were principally the University College of the West Indies, the West India Regiment, the Federal Public Service, and various financial and advisory services. Many of the most important federal powers are shared with the territorial governments, although where there is inconsistency federal laws prevail over territorial laws. There is no exclusive territorial list. In this as in many other respects, the West Indian constitution conforms to the Australian model. The residual powers reserved to the territories embrace such matters as agriculture, primary and secondary education, housing, social welfare, and the police.

A striking feature of the distribution of powers is its flexibility. Not only is there a lengthy and impressive joint legislative list, but the sphere of concurrent jurisdiction can be extended by the voluntary delegation of exclusive federal powers to the territories, or vice versa. A further stipulation provides that, in the event of a national emergency, the federal government can invade the legislative field of the territories, and in the case of a local state of emergency, territorial governments can invade the normal legislative jurisdiction of the federal government. Additional constitutional flexibility is permitted by the provision authorizing governments to spend their money as they wish, whether or not they have the necessary legislative competence.

The federal government is not yet ready to assume full re-

[6] *Report of the British Caribbean Standing Closer Association Committee, 1948–49*, Col[onial] No. 255 (London, H.M. Stationery Office, 1950), p. 17.

sponsibility for many concurrent functions. It may eventually take over all of them, but for some time to come most of them are likely to remain with the units. Thus, for instance, there are still no West Indian stamps, but only stamps issued by Jamaica, Trinidad, etc. Nor is there yet any single West Indian currency. The eastern territories (including British Guiana) unified their currencies in 1951, but both Jamaica and British Honduras have refused to adopt the West Indian dollar. The territorial governments may still legislate for marriage, to meet the wishes of the Hindus and Moslems of Trinidad, and for divorce, at the insistence of the Roman Catholics of St. Lucia. Even matters of such national concern as civil aviation, television, and atomic energy are on the concurrent list. So are customs and excise duties and control of the movement of persons between territories. The last items are of such vital importance to the future of the federation that they merit special attention.

The problem of internal immigration barriers arises from the fact that Jamaica, Barbados, and most of the smaller islands are seriously overpopulated, whereas Trinidad, and perhaps British Guiana and British Honduras, can absorb modest increases. The 1953 London conference decided that there should be no restrictions on migration "on economic grounds." This formula, which did not go far enough to suit Barbados, was far too radical for Trinidad. However, a 1955 Conference on the Movement of Persons worked out an acceptable compromise which in effect shelved the issue. The preamble to the constitution still calls for "the greatest possible freedom of movement of persons," but implementation of this principle was postponed for at least five years. Territories which now restrict immigration may continue to do so, though after 1963 only with the consent of the federal legislature. Acceptance of a possible federal veto of her immigration policy was part of the price Trinidad paid to secure the federal capital.

The West Indies is also unique among federations in that political union has preceded economic union. This is particularly surprising in view of the fact that, as the Croft Commission pointed out in 1958, "economic functions . . . will occupy a larger place in the total field of Federal responsibilities than in other Federations." Indeed, for a time, it was anticipated that a customs union might emerge even before the establishment of a federation. The McLagan Commission in 1950 called for the creation of a full customs union "at the earliest opportunity." "The obstacles to be overcome," it added, ". . . are so few and the desire for an early measure of fiscal and economic unity so general that anything in the nature of a transitional period is neither necessary nor expedient." But while the technical aspects of a West Indian customs union have been exhaustively investigated by two expert commissions, no negotiations between the various territories took place until very recently. Beyond acceptance of the general principle, there has been little agreement on the degree of integration desired, the level of the common tariff, or the timetable for its implementation. The sharpest division of opinion is between Jamaica, which is deliberately pursuing a protectionist policy as a stimulus to industrialization, and Trinidad, which has the lowest rates of duty in the federation.

Closely related to the customs union issue is the question of federal finance. As already indicated, during the first few years, at least, the federal government is expected to assume a much smaller share of the total responsibilities of state than is usual in a federation. Even so, advisers on the federal financial structure seriously understimated the likely costs of these minimum federal services. From the start, the federal government found itself in an impossible financial position, with no powers of taxation and a mere pittance to spend, a situation which led the finance minister to describe himself as "the only Minister of Finance without funds."

It was expected—too optimistically, as events have proved— that for the first five years receipts from customs and excise duties at prescribed maximum rates on gasoline, cigarettes, rum, and other alcoholic beverages would be adequate for federal needs. What is more, a ceiling of W.I. $9,120,000 (U.S. $5,320,000) was placed on the amount that the central government could thus collect, any excess being passed on to the units. As a matter of fact, instead of raising the money directly, the federal government imposes a mandatory levy on the territorial governments, each being assessed the proportion of the total which such duties are estimated to yield in that unit. This amounts to a fixed 43.1119 percent in the case of Jamaica and 38.6252 percent in the case of Trinidad. Trinidadians thus contribute nearly twice as much per capita as Jamaicans, though to judge from the volume of Jamaican complaints one would imagine that the position was reversed. The only other significant sources of revenue are small contributions from non-federated territories earmarked for certain common services, and currency profits (or losses). As a result, ordinary expenditure in 1959 was a mere U.S. $6,000,000. More than half of this was in the form of fixed commitments, nearly 30 percent of the federal budget being a grant to the University College of the West Indies. By comparison, ordinary expenditures in Trinidad during 1959 amounted to U.S. $65,000,000.

As the financial situation worsened, the federal government became increasingly desperate. Sir Grantley Adams even went so far as to claim, in September, 1958, that after 1963 the federal government could impose income taxes retroactive to 1958. This remark precipitated a major constitutional crisis. Norman Manley, chief minister of Jamaica, and leader of Adams's party, feared that Adams's statement would undermine efforts to attract foreign investment to Jamaica with offers of tax holidays and other concessions—and consequently might permit his opponents to triumph in the critical Jamaican elections of July, 1959. "When the time comes for the Constitution to be reviewed," he retorted angrily, "Jamaica will withdraw from the Federation unless her interests are fully protected." At the same time the opposition party called for "a new constitution" which would specifically and permanently deny to the federal government any power "to impose retroactive taxation and legislation," to interfere in any way with the tariff structures of any unit territory without its consent, or "to impose any taxes of any kind" without the consent of the territories.[7] Although this resolution was defeated, the threatened secession of more than half of the federation's area and population was not a matter to take lightly.

The emergence of Manley as a protagonist of "states' rights" in The West Indies occasioned consternation in federalist circles, in view of the fact that he had for twenty years been a leading advocate of federation. Part of the explanation is that he was forced by political expediency to appear as uncompromising as the opposition in his defense of Jamaican interests. However, there is more to it than this. Initially, the

[7] *The Parliamentary Debates,* 30th Sitting, Wednesday, 10th December, 1958, cols. 1483–84.

great appeal of federation was that it would speed up economic development and make independence possible. But during the past few years Jamaica has made rapid strides towards self-government and industrialization on her own. In the process, vested political and economic interests have emerged which now see themselves threatened by any federal centralization of power. Besides, to most Jamaicans the federation seems politically as well as geographically remote. The absence of Manley and Bustamente from the federal parliament has not helped to give Jamaicans a sense of belonging.

The establishment of a *modus vivendi* between Jamaica and the federal government which will keep Jamaica's separatist tendencies from assuming dangerous proportions is perhaps the greatest challenge faced by The West Indies. Indeed, with Manley threatening to "get out" unless Jamaica's industrial and economic growth is safeguarded, and Williams of Trinidad demanding "either a strong independent Federation with all of us, or a weak Federation without Trinidad and Tobago," many observers have felt that the infant federation was headed for the rocks. On more than one recent occasion, as the minister of finance has observed, the federation has seemed to be on "the very lip of near certain disaster."

VII

Owing to the parochialism of The West Indies, nationalism there has been less militant than elsewhere. Yet West Indians do insist on their right to full control of their own affairs. In 1958 it was generally assumed that The West Indies would not attain independence until after the end of the five-year transitional period in 1963. At that time, the federal government could, if it wished, eliminate internal immigration barriers, free itself from the crippling effect of the ceiling on customs receipts, and impose income and corporation taxes. However, events in The West Indies and elsewhere have led to demands that the drive towards autonomy be accelerated.

One problem still to be settled is whether an independent West Indies can expect the continuance of the direct British grants-in-aid on which she now greatly depends. During the five-year period 1959–63, these are to amount to U.S. $5,000,000 a year, in the form of subsidies to meet the deficits in the local budgets of seven smaller territories, and in addition an average of nearly U.S. $9,000,000 a year in Colonial Development and Welfare funds. Not so long ago, political independence would have required financial independence. This principle has been violated frequently since the Second World War, most recently in the case of Sierra Leone. But as late as 1956 the official British position was that a state should not rely "for its existence," as opposed to improving its economic situation, on outside help; The West Indies should be able "to stand on its own feet economically and financially" and "finance its administration" before it became independent.[8]

When this is likely to be is not yet clear. Britain has promised to subsidize the administrative budgets of the weaker units for a ten-year transitional period, although federal independence is hardly likely to be delayed that long. At one time the Federal Labour Party was pledged to the attainment of independence by 1963, but many now consider this date unacceptably late. With many less developed countries achiev-

[8] *Report by the Conference on British Caribbean Federation Held in London in February, 1956,* Command Paper No. 9733 (London, H.M. Stationery Office, 1956), p. 4.

ing independence in Africa, West Indian leaders face increasing pressure to achieve early independence.

This essay has dwelt on some of the difficulties and dangers which beset the West Indian nation. But the ledger also has a positive side. While democratic regimes have collapsed in almost all the newly independent countries of Asia and Africa, parliamentary government still flourishes in The West Indies. Frail as it is, a working two-party system does exist. Race relations in The West Indies are occasionally strained, but there has been no bitter communal strife. Nor has The West Indies a linguistic problem, such as has plagued the countries of southeast Asia, or the complications of tribalism which exist in Africa. Far away from the main areas of world strife, The West Indies is largely free of the cold war pressures which have bedeviled Asian democracy. Finally, there are the West Indian people themselves, who express their faith in the national motto: "To Dwell Together in Unity."

The Social Background of

West Indian Federation

DAVID LOWENTHAL

In 1957 a Jamaican cartoonist drew a coat of arms for the new
West Indian federation. It is a circlet surmounted by two sea-
horses and bound together by sheaves of sugar cane and by
the motto "For All Togetherness." Two palm trees on a sandy
beach fill the circle, around which are scattered various West
Indian fruits and a pair of machetes. In the center is a shield,
emblazoned with a shovel, a rake, and some more fruit—a
pineapple, a banana, a coconut. On top of the shield—directly
between the machetes—is a baby. After all, the artist explains,
"One of our principal products is babies."

A great many babies are born in The West Indies: 125,000
each year in a population of three and a quarter million. According to most standards The West Indies are desperately
overpopulated: on the average there are 400 people to a
square mile, and only half an acre of cultivable land per per-

I am indebted to Michael G. Smith and Lloyd Braithwaite for pains-
taking criticism and detailed suggestions, as well as for much of the basic
research on which this study relies. For their helpful comments on various drafts of this paper I am also grateful to George E. Cumper, David
T. Edwards, Sidney Greenfield, Richard Hartshorne, Donald Q. Innis, and
Vera Rubin.

son. Plantations hold much of the best terrain; only a few of the hundreds of thousands of small farmers own or rent enough land to support their families. For the rest, additional outside work is essential. But one out of five in the agricultural labor force is unemployed and mechanization constantly eliminates more jobs, while seasonal underemployment is practically universal; outside of agriculture there are opportunities for very few. The number of people who have left the islands in search of a livelihood has mounted from year to year. Net emigration in 1956—principally to England—was more than 30,000: that is, one out of every hundred West Indians, by and large the best trained and the most enterprising. Seven years of migration have brought 150,000 West Indians to England. There are now more West Indians in England than in any one of the seven smallest of the ten federating territories.

But emigration is at best a temporary alleviant. Migration to the United Kingdom cannot long continue at the present rate—20,000 in the first six months of 1960—because opportunities as well as hospitality in England are limited; and there is hardly anywhere else for West Indians to go in a world which discriminates against Negroes. Yet even in the peak year, 1956, emigration drained off less than one third of the natural increase—the excess of births over deaths.

The rate of natural increase is, beyond doubt, of crucial importance. No matter how crowded a country may be, if the population remained stable some economic plan could probably be worked out which would eventually take up the slack in employment. But when the number of people constantly increases, production must continually be accelerated just to maintain the original level of living. The faster population rises, the more difficult it is, financially, socially, and techno-logically, to achieve economic progress.

Properly to develop an agricultural economy like that of The West Indies would require, the economist J. J. Spengler estimates, an annual investment of 14 percent of the national income where population increases by one percent a year and an investment of 20 percent of the national income where population increases by two percent.

That is below the present rate in The West Indies. In 1960 there are three and a quarter million West Indians; there will be four and a quarter million by 1970. Without emigration, the annual population increase would be three percent. Such rapid growth is a relatively recent phenomenon: a generation ago the rate of increase in the British Caribbean was only one percent a year. Medicine and sanitation have prolonged life, notably by reducing infant mortality; and the annual death rate fell from 24 per thousand in the 1920s to 10 per thousand in the 1950s. Other circumstances have increased the birth rate from 35 per thousand fifteen years ago to nearly 40 per thousand today. Both of these trends seem certain to continue: the death rate may drop as low as seven per thou-sand, below the United States rate (7.8); while birth rates in some of the territories have already exceeded 50 per thou-sand, double the United States rate. Fertility—that is, the number of children per adult in the reproductive years—is also rising. An unfortunate consequence of the increasing gap between births and deaths is the extreme youth of the population: 40 percent of all West Indians are below the age of fifteen, compared with 30 percent in the United States. This places a heavier burden on wage earners. Though the labor force is too large for the number of jobs available, it is a relatively small proportion of the total population which has to be fed, housed, clothed, and educated.

But this statement of the problem tells nothing specific about The West Indies. Comparable dilemmas perplex most so-called underdeveloped countries, especially tropical colonies and ex-colonies dependent on agricultural exports. Just how inadequately such data describe West Indian conditions becomes obvious when one examines the facts island by island. All sorts of paradoxes confound simple correlations between overpopulation and vital statistics. The territory whose population has grown most rapidly is by far the richest and has few emigrants; that is, Trinidad, which between 1844 and 1955 increased tenfold, three times as much as the rest of the British Caribbean. The most densely inhabited island, Barbados, with 1,400 people per square mile, almost four times the federal average, has next to the lowest rates of fertility, birth, and natural increase. The territories most affected by emigration have, by and large, lower birth rates and less poverty than the others. Unemployment is more widespread in Dominica and St. Lucia, where there is considerable uncultivated arable land, than in many islands where land is scarce. Land hunger is perhaps most acute in British Guiana, which has more available fertile soil than any of the islands. Infant mortality, a classical index of "backwardness," has long been disproportionately high in Barbados, which has the best schools, the highest literacy rate, and the most doctors per capita in the British Caribbean.

These paradoxes give some idea of the range of special conditions in the various territories, conditions that make demographic generalization difficult and sometimes meaningless.

II

No doubt overpopulation is a grave problem for the federation as a whole. But serious as it is, it may not be the main problem The West Indies face. More important than vital statistics is the question of national identity. It matters less how many West Indians there are than *what* they are. In the words of an eminent West Indian educator, "We are still unsure of ourselves, still feeling our way to Nationhood—still trying to discover what we are like—what makes us characteristically West Indian, . . . what is the essence of our West Indianness." [1] The difficulty is that the people who inhabit these scattered islands are just beginning to become a nation; they are, as yet, hardly West Indian at all.

To be sure, there are West Indian cricket teams; there are West Indian students in Montreal, West Indian businessmen in New York, West Indian emigrants in London and Birmingham. There are even West Indian political parties, a prime minister, and a cabinet. But most of these are only superficially or intermittently West Indian. As a British journalist noted, "only when the West Indies cricket team is playing do the islanders from the Windwards and Leewards, from Jamaica, Trinidad and Barbados, recognize themselves as 'West Indians.'" [2] At other times they are very particularistic islanders.

This goes much further than the comparable situation in many other countries. People in the United States are New Yorkers, Californians, Iowans, Texans, and the like as well as Americans. Their various allegiances overlap but do not, for

[1] H. W. Springer, "On Being a West Indian," *Caribbean Quarterly*, III (1953), 181.
[2] "The Caribbean Birthday," *New Statesman*, LV (1958), 397.

the most part, conflict. But in The West Indies regionalism is divisive. Each island is jealous of the others. Physical insularity not only aggravates inter-island differences; it also intensifies a sense of belonging within each island, whatever its size.

In a study of the battle for the federal capital site, I analyzed the self-images and conflicting stereotypes of the three major territories, Jamaica, Trinidad, and Barbados. Federation has intensified their parochialism. The premier of Jamaica, who is also president of the majority West Indian Federal Labour Party, in 1957 complained that there were no steady voices to build up consciousness of West Indian nationhood; in 1959 he threatened to lead Jamaica out of the federation because the federal prime minister—his own party vice president—recommended federal tax powers. The two major political parties of Jamaica recently competed for votes by virtually disowning the federation, and the constitutional conference of September, 1959, was widely headlined as "Jamaica against the Rest." The Jamaican disenchantment can be explained, in part, by the inequities in representation and the electoral setback that gave Jamaica so little voice in the first federal government, by Jamaican fears that customs union and federal taxation might cripple her own development program, and by Premier Manley's own early withdrawal from the federal arena and, hence, from federal leadership. But back of all this lies a question of ultimate goals. Is Jamaica any better off, bound to nine distant and mostly poverty-stricken partners in a federation of three million, than she would be going it alone with half that population? It might be argued that Jamaican leaders ought to have considered this question in 1956. But at that time West Indian nationalism looked to most of them like a pleasant adjunct rather than a perplexing alternative to Jamaican self-government.

Nor is Trinidad without new grievances. Long a magnet for small islanders, Trinidad has with some alarm seen 10,000 of them enter within the last two years. To stem this influx and make federation work, maintains Premier Williams, economic development of the Windwards and Leewards is essential. Failure to embark on this policy, general lack of strength at the federal center, delays in pressing for independence, above all, federal unwillingness to take a strong stand on Chaguaramas—the U.S.-leased naval base in Trinidad, selected as the federal capital site, which America intends to keep until 1977—these are the ostensible grounds for Williams's threat, in March, 1960, to withdraw Trinidad from the federation: "Let me state the alternatives bluntly—either a strong independent Federation with all of us, or a weak Federation without Trinidad and Tobago." And on April 22, 1960, the second anniversary of federation, he conducted a ritual burning of the federal constitution, as "colonialism, and nothing but colonialism. We in Trinidad and Tobago . . . demand . . . either Independence or no Federation."

For Barbados federation now poses fewer special problems than for any other territory. This is a consequence partly of Barbados's intermediate size, partly of her position as headquarters for inter-island trade, partly of the fact that, as one Barbadian journalist put it, "most Barbadians tend to regard the Federal government as specifically theirs because of the leadership of their own Sir Grantley Adams as Federal Prime Minister."[3] Adams is an astute politician. But he continues

[3] George Hunte, "Political Advance in Barbados," *New Commonwealth*, XXXVII (1959), 685.

on many occasions to speak from the Barbadian viewpoint rather than from that of The West Indies. "Barbadians are the most intelligent and industrious people in the West Indies," he remarked, in a speech in New York late in 1959: "Trinidadians prefer to sing calypsoes than to work. Fifty percent of Jamaica is illiterate."

Each of the smaller islands also has special characteristics, a unique self-image, and a particular view of all the others. The "small islanders," the inhabitants of the seven territories in the Windwards and Leewards, have some mutual interests: a man may call himself a small islander when contrasting his poverty, cordiality, or some other supposedly lamentable condition or desirable character trait with those of Jamaicans, Trinidadians, or even Barbadians. But group identification goes no further. For the most part, it is every island for itself; the economic and social structure and political circumstances of each are unrelated to those of any other.

In theory, the small islands stand to benefit most from federation, for they could hardly expect to become, or survive as, independent political units in the modern world; and they have, in fact, received most of the apparent benefits: a disproportionate share of the legislative power, all of the key cabinet posts, the bulk of the current Development & Welfare grants, and the virtually undivided attention of the federal ministries and advisers. Nevertheless, they remain highly dubious about the advantages of federation. These doubts principally concern the wisdom of their exchanging a generous master in Whitehall for an arbitrary or impotent one in Port of Spain; suspicions that the larger islands lack a truly sympathetic understanding of their circumstances and needs; and a fear that their economic salvation, if forthcoming at all, may be purchased only at the sacrifice of all local perquisites and control over education, civil service, and legislation generally.

Federation would be advantageous, according to one commentator, S. G. Fletcher of the Jamaica *Gleaner,* writing in January, 1959, if it accomplished the following: (1) promoted more rapid development than the units could achieve separately; (2) made self-government less expensive than it would be if, for instance, each of the constituent units had to supply ambassadors, trade commissioners, and armies; (3) made West Indians more of a force in world affairs; (4) improved civil service by widening opportunities for good men who had hitherto been confined to their own islands; (5) provided more higher education than the separate units could afford; (6) safeguarded West Indians against dictatorships on the models of Haiti or the Dominican Republic. These would indeed be substantial benefits. The question is, will the prospects for them justify, to West Indians, sacrifice of the self-determination and autonomy that each island holds so precious? At a meeting of the federal Regional Council of Ministers, in January, 1959, representatives from all the unit governments defeated the prime minister's proposal for an economic plan, and hailed their "victory" over the promulgation of *any* federal policy.

Increasingly dubious about the material advantages of union, some West Indian nationalists feel it was a mistake in any case to emphasize economic progress as the driving force of federation. According to Frank Hill, a Jamaican, "our minds dragged our hearts into it." Another observer comments, "It was an unfortunate result of the British Government's encouragement of Federation that it made Federalism remunerative to its apostles." Material self-interest does not inspire peoples to become one nation: "A profound conviction that man does not live by bread alone, but by hamburgers as well, does not provide the drive for a national movement. Economic motivation is not enough."[4] Other motives—self-respect, a sense of national identity—are, indeed, more compelling.

But regionalism is only one aspect of the problem of national identity. Most of the people who are consciously West Indian—cricketers or students or cabinet ministers—are among or close to the elite. Many of them are relatively well off, well educated, and fairly well traveled, with a wide circle of acquaintances in other islands: whatever their own local ties, they share certain aspirations with other West Indians. But these aspirations are beyond the reach of most people. The West Indies is often called a plural society; that is, different segments of the population, divided by class, race, religion, language, and other criteria, tend to adhere to divergent and often antithetical behavior and goals.[5] Profound conflicts of interest within each territory may in one way promote a type of federal amity: a middle-class Jamaican feels more at home with educated Trinidadians than with lower-class people in his own island, and indigenous working-class culture is much the same in all The West Indies. But uniformity is not unity; at bottom, internal pluralism discourages nationalism and impedes any viable inter-island amalgamation.

These social differences are doubly difficult to surmount because most of the milieus within which West Indians must come to terms with each other are isolated small islands, with perhaps ten to a hundred thousand people. As I have tried to

[4] "The Economics of Nationhood—Towards a Federal Economy," *West Indian Economist,* II (No. 5, November, 1959), 20.

[5] See "Social and Cultural Pluralism in the Caribbean," *Annals of the New York Academy of Sciences,* LXXXIII (1960), 761–916.

demonstrate in another connection, groups of this size face many unusual handicaps: a "colonial" relationship with some larger island or with the federal government; a shortage of trained men and of leaders for both federal and local positions; a lack of cultural focus; and a narrow, conservative outlook, with a sometimes pathological sensitivity to criticism, exacerbated by small-island feuds and a claustrophobic absence of privacy.[6]

III

Economic goals may not provide sufficient incentive for West Indian nationhood. All the same, the gravest obstacle to West Indianism is, perhaps, poverty. Whatever local allegiances Jamaicans, Barbadians, or Grenadians may profess, most of them are alike in being underprivileged. Ask a West Indian what he is: nine out of ten might well say, "I am poor." This may, of course, be a plea for help or sympathy; but it is primarily a simple statement of perceived fact. Despite twenty years of undoubted improvement, poverty is still the common lot in every island, even Trinidad. Not only the unemployed know poverty. Field hands on sugar plantations, in islands where work and earnings are concentrated in a four-month crop season, call the rest of the year "hard times," for the best of reasons. There are also the over-employed, domestics who have few hours free from toil.

The mean per capita Jamaican income in 1959 was U.S. $322; but more than half the rural households in Jamaica had incomes of less than U.S. $210 in 1955. In the small islands

[6] David Lowenthal, "The Range and Variation of Caribbean Societies," in *ibid.*, p. 789.

wages are still lower. Agricultural workers in Montserrat went on strike in 1957; a board of enquiry issued a report which forced estates to raise the minimum daily wage for field labor from the U.S. equivalent of 66½¢ to 78¢ a day for men and from 45½¢ to 52½¢ for women. To be sure, tenants are often permitted to raise produce and keep livestock on their few square yards of house plots, or they receive free fuel, grass, or pen manure; such perquisites, a proprietor in Grenada estimated in 1938, were worth about twopence a day per laborer. The cost of living is not comparably low; rent for a small room in the poor quarter of Kingston—with no water, no plumbing, no electricity after ten P.M.—may cost U.S. $7.00 a month or more.

Working or idle, most West Indians can afford only the meanest accommodation, the poorest clothes, the most meager and monotonous diets. Families of six or eight or more live in small one- or two-room shacks, sometimes of wood, but often of tarpaper, cardboard, old kerosene tins, straw, and mud; water supplies and outhouses may be far away. Clothing is often ragged to the point of disintegration. Meals include little fresh meat or dairy produce and few fresh vegetables; diseases caused by vitamin deficiencies, from beri-beri to kwashiakor (severe protein malnutrition), are common among the poor.

Poverty is still the basic fact of West Indian life. People who are face to face with hunger have neither time nor energy for national loyalties, if they are aware of them at all. The average West Indian has too little stake in his society to become a West Indian citizen overnight, even though he now elects his own government. National ideals are of small use to those without property or status.

IV

Status in the West Indies is still linked with color or race. To say "I am poor" is almost the same as to say "I am black"; the phrase "We, the poor people" is an abbreviation for "We, the poor people descended from Africans." [7] To be poor, in West Indian eyes, is to be black; to be white is to be rich; and to be colored is to be somewhere in between, relatively well-off, middle-class.

In the West Indies color is not mainly a matter of genealogy, as it is in the United States, where everyone with any Negro forebears is by definition, often by statute, a Negro. Nor is color just a matter of skin pigmentation; it includes a constellation of other features, with "blackness" ascribed to qualities thought to be African and "whiteness" to those considered European. But color is more than physiognomic; it also depends on the company one keeps, hence the remarks Lloyd Braithwaite calls typical of working-class Trinidadians: "I don't like too many dark people around me," and "I want somebody to lighten up my complexion."

In the final analysis, as M. G. Smith shows, in his *Framework for Caribbean Studies,* color is a matter of culture. Whatever their appearance, middle-class people tend to be considered—and to view themselves as—"colored," while lower-class folk, especially in rural areas, are called "black." In Trinidad, Braithwaite reports in his study of that island, owing to inter-marriage the white group includes some people who "bear fairly marked Negroid characteristics but are by definition white; . . . the term 'Trinidad white' is used

[7] Andrew C. Pearse, "West Indian Themes," *Caribbean Quarterly,* II (No. 2, 1952), 17.

[to indicate] that the person described is not really white but passes for white in Trinidad society." [8]

Many colored people are as wealthy as some whites; many black people hold high political office; social mobility is probably increasing in most of the islands. Nevertheless, it is still true that black folk in The West Indies are generally the poorest and have the lowest status; the small, but increasingly important, middle class is chiefly composed of colored people and special minorities; while the upper class—with the most money, the highest status, and the greatest power—is chiefly confined to a small group of whites and near-whites. Racial composition and social situations vary from island to island; there are many "poor whites" in Barbados who are not considered upper class, while in Grenada and Dominica, where whites are few, the local elite is predominantly light-colored. But these are minor variations within the general social alignment of classes. As in post-revolutionary Haiti, so in The West Indies: "Tout' nèg' riche c'est mulât', tout' mulât' pauv' c'est nèg'" (Every rich Negro is a mulatto, every poor mulatto is a Negro).

This hierarchy deeply influences the West Indian personality. The whole social fabric is partly knit together by intermarriage, by acculturation, by assimilation; there is a color-class continuum. And there is one almost universal West Indian value: almost everyone would like to be more white—to be, as Braithwaite quotes from a letter a dark-skinned girl wrote to a Trinidad official, "relieved of the grief of being a Negro." Nor are class divisions—especially in Jamaica and Trinidad—as evident or as rigid as they once were. But to the

[8] Lloyd Braithwaite, "Social Stratification in Trinidad," *Social and Economic Studies,* II (Nos. 2 and 3, 1953), 132, 88.

extent that clear-cut differences can be identified, upper-, middle-, and lower-class social organization as well as material culture are strikingly disparate. Each section of the population tends to have different goals and ideals, even when certain values seem to coincide. Marital patterns and attitudes illustrate the complexity of the situation. Marriage is the rule in the upper and in the middle class, but the former follow contemporary Western behavior models, while the latter display Victorian attitudes toward women and matrimony. People in the lower classes establish unions outside marriage at least until middle or old age. Since the lower class is by far the largest, more than two thirds of the children born in The West Indies are illegitimate.

For a long time this state of affairs was viewed, especially by whites, as a feature, or even a proof, of "Negro promiscuity." Before emancipation it was convenient to think that Negroes preferred ephemeral unions; heavy infant mortality, for example, could thus be blamed on the customs or morals of the slaves rather than on the neglect of the planters. "The frequent shifting of the connection between the sexes," wrote a Jamaican doctor in the late eighteenth century, caused many children to be "lost through neglect and want of maternal affection, which mothers seldom retain for their offspring of a former husband." But attempts to restrain "licentious intercourse" by the introduction of marriage "would be utterly impracticable and perhaps of dangerous consequence," he went on, "as these people are universally known to claim a right of disposing of themselves . . . according to their own will and pleasure." [9]

[9] "Report of Hygienic Circumstances," in S. Fuller, *The Code of Laws for the Government of Negro Slaves in the Island of Jamaica* (London,

Such rationalizations as these have given way to a variety of conflicting explanations. Following M. J. Herskovits, some anthropologists maintain that the mother-centered West Indian family, in which the father plays a minor role, derives from West African social organization. Other scholars find answers in the circumstances of slavery: twice as many men as women were brought from Africa, existing families were broken up, slaves were forbidden to marry, permanent liaisons were discouraged. Still other students link family patterns to present-day economic opportunity and social function.

But marriage is in fact regarded as the ideal, if not the norm, by almost all West Indians. It is also far more common than the illegitimacy rate would lead one to believe. That two thirds of all children are born out of wedlock is an indication not that the parents oppose marriage, merely that they cannot yet afford it. In many cases, weddings celebrate the birth of grandchildren. Almost half the women in Jamaica over the age of forty-five are married, and 80 percent of all West Indians over sixty-five. Marriage demands responsibilities which most people cannot fulfil until late in life. It is felt that a man ought not propose marriage unless he owns his own home and can afford the considerable cost of the wedding celebration; and many think it improper for a married woman to go out to work, or even to have to do her own housework.

In rural Jamaica, as Edith Clarke has shown in *My Mother Who Fathered Me,* people do or do not marry according to their economic ability to live up to these requirements. Thus, in a relatively stable community which prospers on the ex-

---

1789), quoted in Heinz Goerke, "The Life and Scientific Works of Dr. John Quier, Practitioner of Physic and Surgery, Jamaica: 1738–1822," *West Indian Medical Journal,* V (1956), 25.

port of citrus and on a mixed livestock economy, marriage is general because most people can satisfy the accompanying status expectations. By contrast, concubinage—often as permanent as marriage but carrying less prestige—is the rule in an isolated, poverty-stricken community growing subsistence crops and foodstuffs for local markets. In a third area, where population and income fluctuate with seasonal work at the nearby sugar estate, family life is unstable, mating tends to be casual and temporary, and most households are dominated by single women. While marriage is almost always thought of as desirable, failure to marry reflects lack of material success, rather than lack of morality; among lower-class West Indians, little stigma attaches to illegitimacy.

To the middle class, however, marriage is a *sine qua non* of respectability. Whatever explanations social scientists may offer, middle-class West Indians still consider concubinage and illegitimacy shameful and wicked. Such a view enhances their own status. On the one hand, they blame the less "conventional" lower class for the image of West Indians which they feel prevails among Europeans. On the other hand, their own respectability helps differentiate them from the lower class. The upper-class white can better afford a broad-minded sexual morality, for his social position is assured; but middle-class people cannot openly condone nonlegal unions, lest they appear to share lower-class "morals" and hence be degraded to lower-class status.

In his studies of Caribbean social structure, M. G. Smith has summarized a number of other dissimilarities of culture and outlook which tend to dictate the views and habits of separate West Indian sections. In upper-class family life, both parents may maintain authority, while the middle class is

typically patriarchal, and the lower class predominantly matri-
archal. The upper class tends to be agnostic and scientific, the
middle class to believe in a morally perfect God who can be
appealed to but not controlled, while the lower class is apt to
practice revivalism and attempt to manipulate good and evil
spirits. Categories of ownership and attitudes toward property
also differ profoundly. In sports, cricket is the sole universal;
the upper class alone plays golf and tennis, while in other
games, teams are aligned more or less by color. Historical
events and contemporary patterns of all kinds are differently
seen and explained by each section of the population.

Because these value systems almost everywhere coexist and
compete, West Indians tend to be preoccupied with status
relationships and with finding moral justifications for their
attitudes and behavior toward persons below and above them
in the social hierarchy. As one woman nostalgically put it,
"one used to be able to go to Government House and be sure
that one would meet no one there who was darker than one-
self." Guest lists nowadays are easier for governors to cope
with, but such a problem as the color of carnival queens still
arouses intense feeling at all levels of West Indian society.

The United States is also a multiracial society, and has,
indeed, more rigid color barriers than those in The West Indies. But there is no comparable cultural differentiation in
America; instead, whites and Negroes each maintain separate
but in many respects similar social hierarchies, with cultural
continuities across the color line at most social levels. Further-
more, the dominant American culture, which enjoys the highest
prestige, is that of the overwhelming majority of the population. In The West Indies, on the other hand, the culture enjoying the greatest prestige is that of a small group of whites;

the Negro majority is, psychologically speaking, a minority. National institutional allegiances can hardly flourish under such conditions. As a West Indian periodical put it:

To most of these people the Law as it stands is an alien thing, not felt as applying to their daily life because there are so many basic points at which it runs counter to their habits of thought. . . . Our legal system, culled largely from the wide experience of another society, has been adjusted to our own by a process of makeshift and on the unspoken assumption that all things are the same here as there, and if they are not, then they ought to be. This effect has permeated the society and conditioned the minds of our leaders.[10]

Because authority is imposed from above by people whose values are different, it is inevitably coercive.

Suspicious of authority, most people also lack the self-respect desirable for self-government. As Braithwaite expresses it in his monograph on Trinidad, the negative self-evaluation of lower-class Negroes leads them to prefer white to colored bosses, whereas people in the middle class are apt to believe that a local man who achieves power will abuse it. Moreover, those who reach positions of authority tend to consider themselves exceptions and to resist the advance of other West Indians.

v

Black and colored West Indians sometimes do express solidarity in a phrase like "we West Indians," or, in Trinidad, "we Creoles." In the local context, both terms ordinarily leave out whites, whether native-born, metropolitan, or foreign, and persons of all other races. The largest minority—about 12

[10] "The Case for Law Reform. 2: The Conditions Affecting Demand," *West Indian Economist*, II (No. 10, April, 1960), 7.

percent of the federal population—is East Indian. Descendants of indentured workers brought to the plantations between emancipation and the First World War, the East Indians are very unequally dispersed. Jamaica has about 20,000; the Windwards have a few thousand; Barbados and the Leewards have hardly any. But in Trinidad there are 330,000 East Indians, 40 percent of the population; and in British Guiana, which is not in the federation but is a federal focus of interest, half the population is of East Indian descent. In these two territories, the term "Creole" is specifically employed to exclude East Indians; elsewhere, "West Indian" is the more general term.

What qualities are associated with "Creole" and with "East Indian"? I do not mean to exaggerate the differences or the antagonisms, which some social scientists regard as superficial, others as fundamental. In many ways the East Indians in Trinidad have become "Creolized" and their mode of life is much like that of other Trinidadians. Even in British Guiana, where ethnic differentiation is somewhat more pronounced, there is a greater similarity in culture between urban middle-class East Indians and colored people, on the one hand, and between rural lower-class Negroes and East Indians, on the other, than between the two segments of the same racial group. And in the smaller islands the East Indians are all but absorbed in the population; except in Trinidad and British Guiana, they scarcely form a separate community.

All the same, the cleavage between East Indians and Creoles in Trinidad and British Guiana is in some ways sharper than the class distinctions that separate white, colored, and black. East Indian-Creole intermarriage and miscegenation are rare; no interstitial mixture exists to channel mobility, transmit customs, or to siphon off hostilities. The relationship of white, colored, and black groups is to some degree symbiotic or parasitic; that of East Indians and Creoles is largely competitive.

Since the 1930s the East Indian standard of living has risen rapidly, and wartime employment opportunities brought many East Indians from the country to the towns. They now participate at every level of the economy. Their success is often resented by Creoles; and the resentment is reciprocated. Power is shifting toward the East Indians, who are more industrious, frugal, and prolific than the rest of the population: East Indian women over the age of forty-five have had on the average 6.7 children, other Trinidadian woman only 4 children.[11] For a time it seemed that Trinidad's East Indians might find union with the overwhelmingly Negro islands too great a sacrifice of the local political powers they seemed certain to gain; and British Guiana's East Indians, already as numerous as and perhaps more powerful than the Creoles, still fear that federation might force them to relinquish their supremacy and might also open up British Guiana to unrestricted Negro immigration from the islands.

East Indian hesitations about federation tend to be construed by Creoles as a lack of loyalty, if not a positive disloyalty, both to The West Indies and to Great Britain. A few politicians in Trinidad have denounced East Indian rivals as agents of a foreign power and have charged that their ultimate aim is to make the island an outpost of Greater India; West Indians in other islands magnify these accusations, not so much because they believe them, or even out of malice toward East Indians, as to score a point against Trinidad. East Indians

[11] G. W. Roberts and L. Braithwaite, "Fertility Differentials in Trinidad" (International Population Conference, Vienna, 1959, Working Paper 16), p. 2.

in The West Indies do take pride in Indian culture and political independence, but not even the most outspoken Indianists envision a joint political destiny with India. Nor do economic opportunities in India tempt Trinidad East Indians to quit the Caribbean.

Personal attitudes arising out of the competition between the two groups are of more fundamental importance. Creoles tend to regard East Indians as power-driven, grasping, avaricious, stingy, suspicious, and secretive; while the East Indian views the Negro as feckless, childish, lazy, vain, wasteful, and pompous. These stereotypes and the corresponding self-images do affect behavior: surveys made by Vera Rubin among secondary school children in Trinidad bring out significant personality differences. East Indians appear to be more concerned with social prestige, more fearful of being victimized, readier to sacrifice immediate gratifications for future goals, and more dependent on external approval. When they fail, Creole students ascribe lack of success to their personal inadequacies, whereas East Indians often blame external circumstances— illness or accident. The role of conscience in guilt involves a similar dichotomy: Creole children feel most ashamed when they *do* something wrong, East Indians when they are *caught* doing something wrong.[12]

Equality of opportunity may, in time, diminish these differences. But as long as the racial stereotypes endure, both Creoles and East Indians will feel threatened, marked out, discriminated against.

Self-derogation operates even when specific West Indian traits are approved of or praised. For example, English colonial

[12] Vera Rubin, "Approaches to the Study of National Characteristics in a Multicultural Society," *International Journal of Social Psychiatry,* V (1959), 20–26.

officials are traditionally more sympathetic to Africans than to Indians. Indians, it is said, are hardworking and ambitious, but calculating and treacherous, while the happy-go-lucky African, who may not have much initiative or skill, is a much nicer person at heart. He may lose the game, but at least he plays it. In many respects this is the Creole's view of himself as distinct from the East Indian in Trinidad and British Guiana. It cripples initiative because it equates the desirable with the inferior, though not to the same extent as the Uncle Tom complex which afflicts many Negroes in the United States.

The West Indian—or Creole—self-image is affected even by the Chinese, the Portuguese, and the Syrians, small as these minorities are. Together they do not account for two percent of the population of any territory, yet they play highly significant economic roles in The West Indies. For the most part they are shopkeepers, retailers, and wholesalers of dry goods: in some islands they virtually monopolize these functions. The Creoles, to some extent, have come to consider these pursuits inappropriate for them, just as in Trinidad and British Guiana they consider most plantation labor demeaning work, fit only for East Indians. In these areas the "typical" Creole is neither estate worker, shopkeeper, nor merchant; he is a small farmer or a city man, preferably a clerk, civil servant, or teacher.

The West Indies is in some respects a mosaic society, like the one Carleton Coon has pictured, in *Caravan,* for the Middle East, where Arabs, Armenians, Turks, Assyrians, Copts, Kurds, and Persians each have particular, highly differentiated roles in the economy. But in The West Indies the Creole is so dominant numerically that he is the West Indian prototype. Thus the "typical" West Indian is one who abjures a whole series of essential occupational roles.

West Indian Creoles sometimes question East Indian loyalty. They themselves are conspicuously loyal to the crown—not to the Colonial Office—and are proud of it. This is natural enough, for by citizenship, language, history, education, and a thousand customs they *are* English. In the Caribbean it is an excellent thing, in their eyes, to be English. It sets them apart from peoples nearby, French or Spanish in tradition, who live under tyranny or anarchy and who lack both common law and imperial ceremony. Pride in being English is not thought inconsistent with demands for self-rule.

It is a revelation for many West Indian visitors to discover that people in England do not consider them English at all. "In my student days," writes H. W. Springer in the article cited above, "it was quite common to meet English people who would ask West Indians to speak in their own language, not knowing that English was the language in general use in the West Indies." That West Indians are not primitive Africans has doubtless become more evident to the English in the last few years, but greater familiarity has not yet induced them to regard West Indians as compatriots.

Mingled with West Indian pride in being English is resentment against metropolitan Englishmen, who, whatever their own backgrounds and whatever their jobs in The West Indies, have a privileged social position by reason of race. Since a white skin benefits the expatriate physician and the expatriate bank clerk alike, West Indians apply the same stereotype to both: they are imperialists, second raters who hold posts and receive salaries that should belong to West Indians, beneficiaries of "the vast system of outdoor relief" the Colonial Office runs for Englishmen at the expense of the impoverished colonies.

British regional differences, like British class lines, are blurred in the West Indies. As Braithwaite notes, distinctions between English, Scottish, Welsh, and even Irish are usually ignored; everyone from Great Britain is considered English. All the same, local nationalism can be useful. One Welsh agricultural economist establishes rapport with West Indian farmers by emphasizing his Welshness; he points out that *his* people have been under English subjugation for even longer than the West Indians.

Specifically English (as opposed, say, to Scottish) qualities do carry weight in certain professions, however. The 1952 conference that set up the British Caribbean Bar Association came close to rejecting West Indians who had qualified at the Scottish Faculty of Advocates and the Bar of Northern Ireland, because "barrister" was defined as a person called to the Bar of England.

Metropolitan influence pervades countless other West Indian institutions and modes of expression. But not everybody is English in the same way. Georgian or Edwardian upper-class models give way to middle-class Victorianism, whereas working-class people generally personify England in terms of the royal family. East Indian Englishness, again, has a flavor all its own.

Some West Indians, however, are not essentially English at all. In Trinidad, Grenada, St. Lucia, and Dominica, many people are more French than English. These four islands all became British colonies only in the late eighteenth century. Trinidad had previously been Spanish, but many French planters had settled there with their slaves; the other islands were French-owned and -occupied. In all of them a French patois survives. In Trinidad, outside of certain remote districts, it is limited to a few words and phrases; in Grenada it is no longer common; but in St. Lucia and Dominica it is the lingua franca, the mother tongue of all but a fraction of the population, and the vehicle of customary law.

The linguistic situation is a handicap for St. Lucians and Dominicans. They get all their schooling in a foreign language —English. Their teachers are conditioned by training and ambition to despise patois. To them, people who speak patois are inferior, even stupid and unteachable. It is no wonder that the illiteracy rate in these two islands is double what it is in the rest. Compensations are few. Since there is almost no literature in patois, which is remote from Parisian French, these islanders have no contact with French culture. But in St. Lucia and Dominica, even in Grenada and Trinidad, people like to consider themselves French in temperament—volatile, imaginative, fun-loving, artistic, generous—by contrast with the more decorous, phlegmatic, dowdy English islanders. There is some truth in the stereotype; perhaps the image has created its own reality. Certainly the English West Indians find the French islanders lacking in those sterling qualities— responsibility, honesty, seriousness of purpose—that they admire in themselves.

The proximity of the French West Indies helps to keep alive this sense of national difference. People and goods move back and forth continually among St. Lucia, Dominica, Martinique, and Guadaloupe. Many St. Lucians emigrate not to England, but to French Guiana, where land is available and the French patois is spoken.

VII

More serious than the English-French division is that between the educated and the uneducated. Primary education is free and, in theory, universal. Except in Barbados and the Leewards, however, one child in six never goes to school. Those who do so, go sporadically; average primary school attendance in Jamaica in 1958 was only 58 percent of all children between seven and fourteen. Most children leave school to start work by the time they are twelve or thirteen; in Jamaica only eight out of a hundred complete the elementary course. Even those who attend more or less regularly learn little beyond the rudiments in the ordinary primary school, which is desperately overcrowded and understaffed.

The main cutoff point, however, is entrance to secondary school. Barely one out of ten primary school graduates who apply for further education gets a scholarship. For every thirty children in elementary schools there is only one in a grant-aided secondary school. Without substantial aid only the wealthy can afford to attend the few secondary schools that exist. Reforms are under way, but less than four percent of the total school enrollment is now receiving secondary education.

What is the nature of the gulf between the educated minority—secondary school and university graduates—and the rest? For most West Indians, schooling is almost the only opportunity to gain wealth, power, and status. Education can be a solvent of social stratification: it weakens caste and color barriers, and it makes achievement rather than origin the main measure of merit.

But education has also become another dividing force. The educated man is remote from the common people, partly because he is expected to be, partly because he prefers it. A village, even a whole island, will be proud when a local boy wins a scholarship; but after he goes away to school local people would be disappointed if he continued to think and behave like themselves. When he comes home on vacation he does not go out into the fields, and when he finishes his training he is not expected to return and share the daily life of his family.

These values the scholar soon adopts. Whatever his early goals—to help his family, to improve living conditions at home, to right social wrongs—success requires that he first gain social as well as intellectual prestige. But what confers prestige? The values of the upper class, which, in turn, are patterned on those of the metropolis. The education West Indians receive—based on British public school models—has little relevance to West Indian affairs. "Secondary education in Barbados," the director of education there complained in 1945, "affords an outstanding example of an educational system completely dominated by external examinations. The curricula of the schools, and the teaching in them, appear to be almost completely controlled by the requirements of examiners three thousand miles away, and the tradition of an eighteenth century classical curriculum." [13]

It is not hard to see how this came about. The schools were at first open only to white children, who learned more or less what upper-class children in England were taught. After emancipation a few colored children were admitted; they

[13] [Howard Hayden], *A Policy for Education, Message from His Excellency the Governor Forwarding a Memorandum by the Director of Education*, Barbados, 1945, p. 5.

naturally took the standards of the white elite as their own. Since prestige also required dissociation from slavery, field labor, and the like, the less practical one's schooling, the higher one's status. Thus West Indian school children learned to despise the customs, traditions, and aptitudes of the common folk—local ways of speaking, music and dance, herbal remedies, anything that might possibly be considered "African." Instead they acquired diluted English cultural standards.

As more West Indians went to school, some governments tried to change education to fit the social structure better. They had no success. Education was the very weapon with which the public at large meant to shatter that social structure; meanwhile, it was the best means of escape for the fortunate few. In fact, this was the primary "function of the school from the point of view of the 'folk'," according to Andrew Pearse, who writes:

However slender the chances may be of . . . rising . . . out of the ranks of the labouring classes, modification of the curriculum, or the curtailment of the amount of time spent in "cultural" subjects is deeply resented. Indeed the idea that the school should try to prepare school children for the life which their parents are forced to lead is still abhorrent.

These attitudes are not merely legacies from slavery. Nothing has happened since emancipation to change the feeling of the lower class that agriculture is the fate of the unfortunate. Except perhaps in Barbados, peasants are harassed by problems beyond their control, and few of them believe that rational planning, thrift, or dogged labor would significantly improve their lot. Not that people entirely reject instruction in needlework, domestic sciences, handicrafts, and horticulture. But, Pearse explains,

Even in practical subjects the demand is for training in techniques not for daily life but ceremonial occasions. . . . An attempt to introduce into the school, and to hold in esteem, traditional cultural forms which make up the lives of the parents would be ridiculed by the parents themselves since they know well from experience it is these very forms which must be shed if the adolescent is to find his way through the narrow gate into a superior social position.[14]

As Lloyd Braithwaite says, "It is easy to laugh at those who spurned the calypso for the English folk song; who listened to Grimm's fairy tales but withdrew with horror at acquaintance with [the West Indian] 'Anansi' and the 'Nansi' story." [15] It is analogous to the situation Aubrey Menen describes in Indian universities, where young men who have never seen spring are examined on English poems about it. But in the local context such preferences are explicable. They show the educated man how far he has come from the origins he despises. The West Indian who returns home after being educated abroad is often shocked by the contrast between his own ideas and standards and those of the common people. A compelling theme of local novelists—Samuel Selvon, Jan Carew—is the reaction of the educated West Indian when faced again with his early associates. He is apt to find their superstition and ignorance particularly repugnant. The worst thing that one highly cultivated Barbadian finds to say about his political enemies is that they are advised by soothsayers.

One aspect of this dichotomy is forms of speech. The problem posed by the French patois in some islands is noted above. In the other islands too there is a gulf separating standard English and the Creole variant spoken by the bulk of the

---

[14] "Education in the British Carribbean: Social and Economic Background," *Vox Guyanae*, II (No. 1, February, 1956), 18, 21–22.
[15] "The Development of Higher Education in the British Caribbean," *Social and Economic Studies*, VII (1958), 55.

population—a difference not only in pronunciation but also in vocabulary and grammar. Standard English, sometimes called "white talk," is spoken regularly only by upper- and some middle-class folk, and not all the time by them; a more or less educated Creole is heard in most homes. But standard English is required in school and standard English alone is legitimate. West Indians are thus in good part bilingual. Yet many educated West Indians revile Creole as a vulgar tongue which debases speakers and listeners alike, not a language at all but a demeaning form of communication, an adjunct to chicanery, laziness, and vice.

This condemnation cannot be dismissed merely as an attempt to moralize status difference. Although vigorous and colorful, Creole has severe limitations. It originated as a makeshift means of contact between master and slave for giving and receiving orders, a deliberate truncation of English designed for illiterates, lacking in nuances, impoverished in the vocabulary and syntax of abstract ideas. To this day it is unwritten, save for poetry and humor of a kind which usually holds up to ridicule both dialect and speaker.

It is little wonder that primary school teachers reacted with scandalized horror to a suggestion that education might begin in Creole. Teachers are, of course, linguistic traditionalists; they are socially ambitious and have a vested interest in "correct" English. But even lower-class folk oppose the use of Creole in school, for they rightly believe that their dialect deprives them of benefits which go to those who are fluent in standard English. A linguistic survey undertaken by the University College of the West Indies was bitterly resented in many quarters, because it seemed to imply that West Indians were different, that is, African, inferior; the middle class, in particular, viewed a sympathetic attitude toward Creole as evidence of a plot to deprive them of proper English and all its associated virtues.

Many West Indians never learn much standard English. But those who do surmount the language barrier suffer a "dichotomy of thought and expression, a split between their native culture and the alien culture they have gone to so much trouble to acquire." They feel obliged to turn their backs upon their homes. The educated, the potential leaders, often take little interest in local affairs; "they will not talk to their own people in their own language but wish only to remain aloof in a middle-class suburb." [16]

One might ask whether educated West Indians can lead a people from whom they feel so alienated. Yet it is by no means only the successful few who are anxious to preserve such distinctions. One commentator notes a "kind of exclusiveness which often invades even the underprivileged who unconsciously fear that anything which extends beyond the very small élite can not be worth fighting for anyway." [17] There may be some virtue in the often-stated opinion that the little money and talent available will be better spent on first-rate training for a few than on third-rate instruction for the many. If the University College of the West Indies were modeled along the lines of the University of Puerto Rico, with service courses for thousands, standards would be so low, it is often said, that self-respecting West Indians would not attend it; the best students would go abroad. But most of the best students go abroad anyway; only a small minority of territorial

---

[16] R. B. Le Page, "The Language Problem of the British Caribbean," *Caribbean Quarterly*, IV (No. 1, January, 1955), 45.

[17] "Education in Barbados," *West Indian Economist*, I (No. 6, December, 1958), 15.

scholarship winners have chosen to go to the University College of the West Indies. The existence of a topflight local university may bolster West Indian prestige, but the residential requirements (nonresident students were first admitted in October, 1960) and the small size and special character of the student body have aroused some misgivings that high standards have perhaps been cherished not only for their own sake, but also to sustain an aristocratic notion that general progress is not really desirable. The vicarious pleasures of the many in the progress of a small elite may not always seem to them, however, a satisfactory substitute for their own advancement. It is not without significance that the first public statement issued by the University College's first West Indian principal, the economist W. A. Lewis, included an announcement that the student body would be increased from 700 to 2,000 within a few years.

VIII

Most of this essay has dealt with features that seem to divide West Indian loyalties, and to show that the federated islanders are something other than West Indians, or are dissatisfied with being West Indians. Yet this is not the whole story. "I am satisfied," wrote a Syrian business leader from Jamaica, after his first tour of the eastern Caribbean, "that we are all one people—a nation divided only by water, but sharing the same national characteristics, ambitions and attitudes in surprisingly high degree." [18] The ferment of self-discovery makes The West Indies an exhilarating place. The emergence of a nation encourages people to turn their hopes into action.

[18] A. E. Issa, *A Survey of the Tourist Potential of the Eastern Caribbean* (The West Indies, Ministry of Trade & Industry, 1959), p. 37.

I have elsewhere compared the political circumstances of the new West Indies with those of the American republic in the 1780s. The West Indian temperament, too, is reminiscent of that of Americans in the early national period. In The West Indies, people are concerned with local matters that they understand and can influence; private citizens have many mutual interests; public passions are easily aroused; warmth, ebullience, extravagant vituperation, and a healthy disrespect for the laws of libel characterize public debate and the press. West Indians still find it easy, as the Trinidadian novelist V. S. Naipaul points out, in an article on literary regionalism in the *Times Literary Supplement,* to be themselves; class behavior may conform to group standards, but private idiosyncrasies are tolerated and individualism is cherished.

Such are the qualities that mark out the West Indian. They are not usually what a man thinks of when he says, "I am a West Indian." But these national self-images too have great value, however little they may yet be realized. Beyond mere pride in nationhood, they convey confidence that the more divisive differences will, in time, be confronted and overcome; that specific local virtues will win general acceptance; and that The West Indies may help to teach the world that despite a heritage of slavery, colonialism, and poverty, a people of varied ethnic backgrounds and social ideals can achieve not only comfortable coexistence but nationhood and a personality.

Table 1. Area, Population, and Vital Statistics

TERRITORY	AREA (in square miles)	POPULATION 1960 (provisional) Total	Percent of W.I.	DENSITY (persons per sq. mile)	PREVIOUS POPULATION 1844	1921	1946	RATE OF INCREASE (annual percent) 1844–1921	1921–1946	1946–1960	VITAL STATISTICS (1956–58 averages) Birth rate	Death rate	Natural increase
Jamaica	4,411	1,606,546	51.6	364	337,433	858,118	1,237,063 b	1.2	1.7	1.6	37.8	9.1	28.7
Trinidad	1,980	825,700	26.5	417	73,023	365,900	557,970	2.1	1.7	2.8	37.0	9.3	27.7
Barbados	166	232,085	7.45	1,396	122,198	156,774	192,800	0.3	0.8	1.3	30.9	10.4	20.5
Grenada	133	88,617	2.85	666	29,650	66,302	72,387	1.0	0.4	1.5	46.5	11.1	35.4
St. Vincent	150	80,005	2.6	532	27,248	44,447	61,647	0.6	1.3	1.9	47.4 c	13.6 c	33.8 c
St. Lucia	233	86,194	2.8	370	20,694 d	51,505	70,113	1.2	1.2	1.5	42.2	13.5	28.7
Dominica	305	59,479	1.9	195	22,469	37,059	47,624	0.6	1.0	1.6	40.0	14.2	25.8
Antigua	170	54,354	1.7	319	36,687	29,767	41,757	−0.2	1.4	1.9	33.3	9.4	23.9
St. Kitts-Nevis-Anguilla	152	56,644	1.8	373	34,927	38,214	46,243	0.1	0.8	1.5	45.1	13.8	31.3
Montserrat	32	12,157	0.4	374	7,365	12,120	14,333	0.6	0.7	−1.2	26.7	11.6	15.1
Cayman Islands	100	7,616	0.2	76	3,000 e	5,253	6,670 b	0.7	1.1	0.8	—	—	—
Turks and Caicos Islands	166	5,716	0.2	34	3,000 e	5,612	6,138 b	0.8	0.4	−0.4	—	—	—
FEDERATION	8,000	3,115,113	100	389	717,704	1,671,071	2,416,400	1.1	1.5	1.8	—	—	—
Br. Virgin Is.	59	7,338	—	124	6,689 f	5,082	6,505	−0.3	1.0	0.9	—	—	—
Br. Guiana	83,000	558,769	—	7	98,133	307,391	375,701	1.5	0.8	2.8	—	—	—
Br. Honduras	8,866	90,343	—	10	10,000 e	45,317	59,220	2.0	1.0	3.1	—	—	—
BR. CARIBBEAN	99,925	3,771,563	—	38	832,526	2,028,061	2,856,800	1.2	1.4	2.0	—	—	—

Sources: 1960 population estimates from The Daily Gleaner (Kingston, Jamaica, August 31, 1960. Other population totals from West Indian Census, Part A: General Report on the Census of Population 9th April, 1946 (Kingston, Jamaica), 1950, and G. W. Roberts, Population of Jamaica, pp. 330–33. Vital statistics from United Nations Population and Vital Statistics Reports, Statistical Papers, Series A, Vol. XII, No. 3, 1 July, 1960, and previous reports, and from scattered territorial statistics.

a Annual percentages based on midyear population estimates. Brought forward to 1960, these estimates exceed the provisional 1960 census totals by the following percentages (approximate): Montserrat, 15; Antigua, Dominica, St. Lucia, 10; St. Kitts, 7; Jamaica, Grenada, St. Vincent, Barbados, 5; Trinidad, 1. The birth, death, and natural increase rates given here may thus be too low by amounts up to these percentages.
b 1943. c 1956 and 1958 only. d 1943. e Estimated. f 1841.

Table II. Trade and Production

TERRITORY	EXTERNAL TRADE (annual averages, 1955–59)			DOMESTIC EXPORTS (1959)		COMMODITY VALUE (percent of total domestic exports, 1958–59)							SUGAR (1960)
	Imports (total value in $1,000 B.W.I.)[a]	Exports (including reexports) (percent of W.I.)	Exports as per-cent of imports	Total Value (in $1,000 B.W.I.)[b]	Per capita value (in $B.W.I.)	Sugar, rum, mo-lasses	Ba-nanas	Ca-cao	Citrus fruits	Cot-ton[c]	Copra, coco-nut oil[c]	Other	Produc-tion in 1,000 tons)
Jamaica	291,795	208,033	31.3	71	216,732	134.91	28	11	1	4	—	—	Bauxite & alumina 46 / Pimento[c] 2	434
Trinidad	362,361	376,408	56.6	104	434,894	526.70	8	—	3	1	—	—	Petroleum & asphalt 82	218
Barbados	67,389	42,164	6.3	63	39,692	170.02	94	—	—	—	—	—	—	154
Grenada	11,377	6,837	1.0	60	7,631	86.11	—	22	36	—	—	—	Nutmeg & mace[c] 40	—
St. Vincent	8,578	5,438	0.8	63	6,486	81.07	—	46	—	—	5	8	Arrow-root[c] 26	4
St. Lucia	8,299	4,776	0.7	57	6,295	73.12	20	55	9	—	—	10	—	5
Dominica	7,896[d]	5,932	0.9	75[d]	6,767	113.77	—	63	—	19	—	5	—	—
Antigua	12,062[e]	6,041	0.9	50[e]	4,819	88.66	76	—	—	—	18	—	—	20
St. Kitts	10,606[e]	9,589	1.4	90[e]	9,193	162.29	94[f]	—	—	—	4[f]	—	—	50
Montserrat	1,359	383	0.1	28	512	42.07	—	—	—	2	82	—	Cattle[e] 7	—
FEDERATION TOTAL	780,851	665,615	100.0	85	733,021	236.32	20	5	2	2	—	—	Petroleum products 48 / Bauxite 14	885

[a] $1.00 B.W.I. = $.59 U.S.
[b] Based on 1960 provisional census totals.
[c] Amounts to less than one percent of total federal exports.
[d] 1957 figures missing; figure given is a four-year average.
[e] 1959 figures partly missing; remainder extrapolated.
[f] Figures for 1959 only.

Sources: The West Indies, Federal Statistical Office, *Monthly Trade Statistics*, II (No. 9, Sept., 1960), Tables 2, 3, 4, and 9 (for columns 1–13). The West Indies, Ministry of Trade and Industry, *Trade and Industry*, Bulletin No. 9 (31st September, 1960), p. 9 (for column 14).

Table III. Finances and Income

TERRITORY	GOVERNMENT REVENUE, 1959		BRITISH GOVERNMENT GRANTS, 1951–60			NATIONAL INCOME, 1957			AGRICULTURAL INCOME, 1957
	Total (in $1,000,000 B.W.I.) [b]	Grants [a] (as percent of revenue)	Total (in $1,000,000 B.W.I.)	Percent of total grants to territories	Per capita annual average (in $B.W.I.)	Total (in $1,000,000 B.W.I.)	Per capita (in $B.W.I.)	Percent of total W.I. income	Percent of gross domestic product
Jamaica	165.9 [c][d]	4.5 [e]	31.5	26	2	821.8	510	54.5	13.8
Trinidad	170.0 [c][d][e]	0.4 [e]	9.1	7	1	471.5	612	31.3	13.7
Barbados	22.6 [d]	3.5	5.0	4	2	100.0	431	6.6	34.3
Grenada	6.9	29.8	6.0	5	7				
St. Vincent	6.0	47.0	12.5	10	16	79.7	244	5.3	42.6
St. Lucia	6.0	36.0	14.5	12	16				
Dominica	5.6	49.2	16.5	13	27				
Antigua	6.7 [e]	27.2 [e]	17.0	14	33	15.9	284	1.1	30.4
St. Kitts-Nevis-Anguilla	5.2 [e]	12.3 [e]	5.0	4	9	15.0	261	1.0	42.6
Montserrat	1.5	70.9	6.5	5	47	2.8	195	0.2	49.4
FEDERATION TOTAL	396.4	5.5	123.5	100	4	1,506.7	491	100.0	16.8
FEDERAL GOVERNMENT TOTAL	11.8	4.0							

[a] Grants include imperial grants-in-aid and Colonial Development and Welfare funds.   [c] Including loans.
[b] $1 B.W.I. = $.59 U.S.   [e] Estimated.
[d] Figures are for fiscal year 1959–60.

Sources: British government grants, 1951–60, from *The Nation* (Port of Spain, Trinidad), July 1, 1960; national income and gross domestic product data from The West Indies, Federal Statistical Office, *National Income Statistics*, No. 1 of 1960: National Accounts of The West Indies, Tables 1B and 4; government revenue figures from territorial estimates and from *The Economics of Nationhood*, Tables I and VII.

A Selected West Indian Reading List

DAVID LOWENTHAL

The books and articles listed below are a small cross section of the voluminous literature on The West Indies now available. They are arranged under the following heads:

1. Government reports and official documents relating to West Indian federation (arranged chronologically).
2. Physical geography (geology, climate, soils, vegetation).
3. History (works concerned mainly with tracing the past, as well as all works published before 1929).
4. Contemporary affairs (politics, economics, society, culture, travel, and other aspects of present-day life).
5. Belles-lettres (novels, short stories, and poetry with West Indian settings).
6. Periodicals and newspapers.

Like most classifications, this one is somewhat arbitrary; some books classified as "Physical geography" are equally "History"; a number of items combine historical and contemporary interests.

The list includes the most important and comprehensive writings on The West Indies, as well as works of more limited scope or significance, chosen to illustrate the range and variety of information available. Good points of departure for reading about The West Indies are the twelve starred books and articles, recent works of broad coverage or vivid interpretation in their respective fields.

Most of the sources listed deal exclusively with The West Indies or its constituent parts, but several of the most interesting compare the federating islands with others nearby, or treat the Caribbean as a whole. A few books and articles on West Indian migrants in

England and on British Guiana, British Honduras, and the British
Virgin Islands—lands outside the federation but closely connected
in other respects—have also been included.

The following sources were particularly useful in the preparation
of this reading list:

American Geographical Society, New York, N.Y. Research Catalogue. A card catalogue of all books, periodical articles, and
maps received by the Society since 1923, divided by areas
(countries and regions) and by topics (subject matter and type
of information).

Canton, E. Berthe. "A Bibliography of West Indian Literature,
1900–1957," *Current Caribbean Bibliography,* VII (1957), 1–56.
Port of Spain, Trinidad, Caribbean Commission, 1960.

Easton, David K. "A Bibliography on the Federation of the British
West Indies," *Current Caribbean Bibliography,* V (1955),
1–14. Kent House, Port of Spain, Trinidad, Caribbean Commission.

Goveia, Elsa V. A Study of the Historiography of the British West
Indies to the End of the Nineteenth Century. (See under "History.")

Hills, Theo. L., comp. A Select Annotated Bibliography of the
Humid Tropics (International Geographical Union, Special Commission on the Humid Tropics). Montreal, Geography Department, McGill Univ., 1960. For data on the British West Indies,
see pp. 149–52, 161–64.

Ragatz, Lowell J., comp. A Guide for the Study of British Caribbean History, 1763–1834, Including the Abolition and Emancipation Movements (Annual Report of the American Historical
Association, 1930, Vol. III). Washington, Gov. Print. Off., 1932.
775 pp.

———— Writings on the Caribbean Dependencies, 1928–1958. Pre-
print edition, 20 November, 1958. 74 pp.

Smith, M. G., comp. Short Bibliography of Literature on Jamaica.
1957. Mimeographed. 7 pp.

West India Reference Library, Institute of Jamaica. Select List of
Works on British West Indian Federation. Kingston, Jamaica,
1957. Mimeographed. 12 pp.

1. GOVERNMENT REPORTS AND OFFICIAL DOCUMENTS
RELATING TO WEST INDIAN FEDERATION

Great Britain. Colonial Office. Report by the Honourable E. F. L. Wood on His Visit to the West Indies and British Guiana, Dec. 1921–Feb. 1922 (Cmd. 1679). London, H.M.S.O., 1922. 101 pp. Recommendations by the future Lord Halifax favoring constitutional advance and union of Trinidad and the Windward Islands, but advising against general federation, owing to economic and cultural diversity, difficulties of communication, and probable public opposition.

Great Britain. Report of the Closer Union Commission (Leeward Islands, Windward Islands, Trinidad and Tobago) (Cmd. 4383). London, H.M.S.O., 1933. 46 pp. Agricultural cooperation stressed, closer association between the Windwards and the Leewards proposed, but federation rejected.

Great Britain. West India Royal Commission (1938–39). Recommendations . . . (Cmd. 6174). London, H.M.S.O., 1940. 30 pp.

Great Britain. West India Royal Commission (1938–39). Report . . . (Cmd. 6607). London, H.M.S.O., 1945. 480 pp.

Great Britain. West India Royal Commission (1938–39). Statement of Action Taken on the Recommendations . . . (Cmd. 6656). London, H.M.S.O., 1945. 108 pp. A study of the economic and social problems of all of the territories, resulting in the unification of some public services and the establishment in 1940 of the Development and Welfare Organization in the West Indies.

Great Britain. Colonial Office. Report on Closer Association of the British West Indian Colonies (Cmd. 7120). London, H.M.S.O., 1947. 44 pp. Memorandum from the Secretary of State for the Colonies to the West Indian legislatures inviting them to debate the issue of federation; resulted in the Montego Bay Conference (1947).

Conference on the Closer Association of the British West Indian Colonies, Montego Bay, Jamaica, 11th–19th September, 1947. London, H.M.S.O., 1948. 2 vols. Pt. 1, Report . . . 1948 (Cmd. 7291); Pt. 2, Proceedings . . . 1948 (Colonial No. 218). The principle of federation accepted; a Regional Economic Committee set up; and a Closer Standing Association Committee composed of territorial representatives established to report on public service and currency unification and on a federal constitution and judiciary.

British Caribbean Standing Closer Association Committee. Report 1948–49. Bridgetown, Barbados, Advocate Co., 1949. 107 pp. The so-called Rance Report (after the chairman of the Committee, Sir Hubert Rance). The first blueprint for the federation, recommending a constitution based on the Australian model.

Great Britain. Colonial Office. British Dependencies in the Caribbean and North Atlantic, 1939–1952 (Cmd. 8575). London, H.M.S.O., 1952. xi, 98 pp. A review of progress since the establishment of the West India Royal Commission of 1938–39.

Great Britain. Colonial Office. The Plan for a British Caribbean Federation: Agreed by the Conference on West Indian Federation Held in London in April 1953 (Cmd. 8895). London, H.M.S.O., repr. 1955. 30 pp. Revision of the Standing Closer Association Committee's report, dealing notably with legislative representation (owing to the nonparticipation of British Guiana and British Honduras), finance, freedom of movement, and constitutional amendment.

Great Britain. Colonial Office. The Plan for a British Caribbean Federation: Report of the Fiscal Commissioner (Cmd. 9618). London, H.M.S.O., 1955. 71 pp. Estimates of federal costs and sources of revenue.

Great Britain. Colonial Office. The Plan for a British Caribbean Federation: Report of the Civil Service Commissioner (Cmd. 9619). London, H.M.S.O., 1955. 76 pp. Deals with the establishment and structure of a federal public service.

Great Britain. Colonial Office. The Plan for a British Caribbean Federation: Report of the Judicial Commissioner . . . (Cmd. 9620). London, H.M.S.O., 1955. 20 pp. Considers the jurisdiction and costs of the federal supreme court.

Great Britain. Colonial Office. Report by the Conference on British Caribbean Federation, Held in London in February 1956 (Cmd. 9773). London, H.M.S.O., 1956. Final ratification of federation by territorial delegates; agreements on hitherto unsettled constitutional, fiscal, administrative, and judicial matters, notably customs union.

Great Britain. Colonial Office. Report of the British Caribbean Federal Capital Commission (Colonial No. 328). London, H.M.S.O., 1956. 48 pp., maps. Recommendation of Barbados, Jamaica, and Trinidad (in that order) as sites for the federal capital, based on various criteria.

Great Britain. British Information Services. The West Indies: a Nation in the Making (Reference Division, I.D. 1282). New York, December, 1957. 56 pp. General survey of the political, economic, and social background of the federation.

The West Indies: Report of the Trade and Tariffs Commission (W.I. 1/58). 2 pts. Bridgetown, Barbados, 1958. Pt. I: 91 pp; Pt. II: 82 pp. Analysis of the establishment of a customs union, its advantages, and its costs.

The West Indies. Federal Information Service. The West Indies 1958. Port of Spain, Trinidad, 1958. 36 pp. General survey on the occasion of the opening of the first federal parliament.

Trinidad and Tobago. Office of the Premier and Ministry of Finance. The Economics of Nationhood (Trinidad, M. 23/59). Trinidad, Gov. Print. Off., Sept. 11, 1959. 48 pp. Buttresses the Trinidadian viewpoint favoring a strong central government for the federation.

Trinidad and Tobago. Office of the Premier and Ministry of Finance. Economic Development of the Independent West Indies Federation; I: The Case for United Kingdom Assistance. Port of Spain, Trinidad, Gov. Print. Off., October, 1960. 59 pp. Survey of the financial needs of the individual territories and the central government, and of the funds available, and recommendations for allocations from U.K. grants-in-aid and Development & Welfare funds.

2. PHYSICAL GEOGRAPHY

Asprey, G. F. "Vegetation in the Caribbean Area," *Caribbean Quarterly*, V (1959), 245–63. General survey of types of plant associations, grouped according to ecological conditions.

Asprey, G. F., and R. G. Robbins. "The Vegetation of Jamaica," *Ecological Monographs,* XXIII (1953), 359–412. A survey of the flora and description of the plant communities of the coast, lowlands, and mountains, with discussions of their ecology and interrelationships.

*Beard, John Stewart. The Natural Vegetation of the Windward and Leeward Islands (Oxford Forestry Memoirs, No. 21). Oxford, Clarendon Press, 1949. 192 pp. The environment, plant geography, and floristic associations of the Lesser Antilles, with detailed descriptions of each of the islands in the chain; many maps and diagrams.

———— The Natural Vegetation of Trinidad (Oxford Forestry Memoirs, No. 20). Oxford, Clarendon Press, 1946. 152 pp. Environmental factors, flora, plant communities, and ecological relationships.

Butterlin, Jacques. La Constitution geologique et la structure des Antilles. Paris, Centre National de la Recherche Scientifique, 1956. 453 pp. Review of the geology of each island and discussion of the various tectonic and geophysical theories put forward to explain Antillean structure and history.

Davis, William Morris. The Lesser Antilles (Map of Hispanic America Publication No. 2). New York, American Geographical Society, 1926. 207 pp. Classic work on the land forms and physiographic history of the island arc.

Doran, Edwin, Jr. "Land Forms of Grand Cayman Island, British West Indies," *Texas Journal of Science,* VI (1954), 360–77. General description, topography, and geomorphic history.

Flowering Trees of the Caribbean. New York, Rinehart, 1951. 125 pp. Thirty paintings by Bernard and Harriet Pertchik; botanical and general information about each species.

Great Britain. Meteorological Office. Aviation Meteorology of the West Indies (Meteorological Reports, No. 22). London, H.M.S.O., 1959. 85 pp. A practical guide to the weather of the West Indies, including the principal meteorological phenomena and aspects of the climate. Contains statistical summaries, by month and year, for air pressure, temperature, humidity, precipitation, cloudiness, and wind directions at fifteen stations in the Caribbean.

Hardy, F., *et al.* "Studies in West Indian Soils," *Tropical Agriculture*, Supplements 3–10, 1931–36. Papers on the soils of Trinidad and Tobago, Jamaica, Antigua, St. Vincent, Grenada, and British Honduras, and their potentialities for various agricultural crops.

Hodge, W. H. "The Vegetation of Dominica," *Geographical Review*, XXXIII (1943), 349–75. Good general description of the environment and plant life of the most rugged of the Lesser Antilles.

Hose, H. R. "The Geology and Mineral Resources of Jamaica," *Colonial Geology and Mineral Resources,* I (1950), 11–36.

Howard, Richard A. "History of the Botanic Garden of St. Vincent, British West Indies," *Geographical Review*, XLIV (1954), 381–93. History and description of the oldest botanical garden in the New World, one instrumental in the introduction of the breadfruit and other economic plants from tropical Asia and the South Seas into America.

———— The Vegetation of the Grenadines, Windward Islands, British West Indies (Contributions from the Gray Herbarium of Harvard University, No. CLXXIV). Cambridge, Mass., 1952. 129 pp. General survey and description of the plant life of each of the island dependencies of Grenada and St. Vincent, together with a systematic account of the flora.

————, and George R. Procter. "Vegetation in Bauxitic Soils in Jamaica," *Journal of the Arnold Arboretum,* XXXVIII (1957), 1–41; 151–69. A thorough study of plant succession and of the effects of bauxite mining on vegetation cover.

Martin-Kaye, P. H. A. Reports on the Geology of the Leeward and British Virgin Islands. St. Lucia, W.I., 1959. 117 pp. Separate studies of each of the islands, with copious maps and sketches.

———— The Water Resources of Antigua and Barbuda, B.W.I. La Penitence, British Guiana, 1956. 109 pp., maps. Covers climate, water supply development, the location and character of wells, springs, and reservoirs, geology, groundwater, and surface drainage.

Meyerhoff, Howard A. "Antillean Tectonics," *Transactions of the*

New York Academy of Sciences, XVI (1954), 149–55. West Indian geologic structure surveyed with brevity and clarity.

Schuchert, Charles. Historical Geology of the Antillean-Caribbean Region, or the Lands Bordering the Gulf of Mexico and the Caribbean Sea. New York, John Wiley, 1935. 811 pp. A basic work on the past and present physical structure of the area.

Soil and Land-Use Surveys. Regional Research Centre of the British Caribbean, Imperial College of Tropical Agriculture, Trinidad. 1. Jamaica: Parish of St. Catherine, 1958; 2. British Guiana: The Rupununi Savannas, 1958; 3. St. Vincent, 1958; 4. Jamaica: Parish of St. Andrew, 1959; 5. British Guiana: Mahdia Valley, Bartica Triangle, Kamarang & Kukui Valleys, A Part of the Upper Mazaruni Valley, 1959; 6. British Guiana: Rupununi Savannas (cont.), Intermediate Savannas, General Remarks, 1959; 7. Jamaica: Parish of Clarendon, 1959; 8. Jamaica: Parish of St. James, 1959; 9. Grenada, 1959; 10. Jamaica: Parish of St. Mary, 1960; 11. Jamaica: Parish of Portland, in press; 12. Jamaica: Parish of Hanover, in press.

Storer, Dorothy P. Familiar Trees and Cultivated Plants of Jamaica: a Traveller's Guide to Some of the Common Trees, Shrubs, Vines and Crop Plants. Kingston, Institute of Jamaica; London, Macmillan, 1958. 81 pp.

Suter, H. H. The General and Economic Geology of Trinidad, B.W.I. 2d ed., with revisionary appendix by G. E. Higgins. London, H.M.S.O., 1960. 145 pp.

Sweeting, M. M. "The Karstlands of Jamaica," *Geographical Journal,* CXXIV (1958), 184–99. Description of the topography and structure of the water-soluble limestone country in north central Jamaica.

Taylor, S. A. G., and L. J. Chubb. "The Hydrogeology of the Clarendon Plains, Jamaica," *Proceedings of the Geologists' Association,* LXVIII (1957), 204–10. The transformation of an arid area in southern Jamaica by irrigation water derived by borehole wells from underground rivers.

Underwood, Garth. "West Indian Reptiles," *Caribbean Quarterly,* III (1953), 173–80. The distribution of lizards and snakes explained historically and ecologically, notably as affected by the introduction of the mongoose.

Watkins, John V. Gardens of the Antilles. Gainesville, Florida, Univ. of Florida Press, 1952. 244 pp. A popular guide to the common garden plants of the West Indies and to the public gardens of the islands.

Zans, V. A. "Bauxite Resources of Jamaica and Their Development," *Colonial Geology and Mineral Resources,* III (1952), 307–33.

—— "Recent Geological Work and Mining Developments in Jamaica: a Brief Review of the Activities during the Last Decade," in Transactions of the 2d Caribbean Geological Conference. Rio Piedras, Puerto Rico, Univ. of Puerto Rico, in press.

3. HISTORY

Acworth, A. C. Treasure in the Caribbean: a First Study of Georgian Buildings in the British West Indies. London, Pleiades Books, 1949. 36 pp., 60 photographs. The development of West Indian architecture in the eighteenth and early nineteenth centuries.

Atwood, Thomas. The History of Dominica. London, 1791. The geography, natural and political history, social conditions, and economic prospects of the island.

Augier, F. R., S. C. Gordon, D. G. Hall, and M. Reckord. The Making of The West Indies. London, Longmans, 1960. 310 pp. A general history focusing particularly on social and economic aspects of life in the British islands and on relationships between the European countries and their West Indian colonies.

Beachey, R. W. The British West Indies Sugar Industry in the Late 19th Century. Oxford, Blackwell, 1957. 189 pp. The state of the sugar industry during the years 1865–1903, when it was confronted with heavy competition and free trade, and when many of the British West Indies turned to other crops.

Bennett, J. Harry, Jr. Bondsmen and Bishops: Slavery and Apprenticeship on the Codrington Plantations of Barbados, 1710–1838 (University of California Publications in History, Vol. 62). Berkeley, Calif., Univ. of California Press, 1958. 176 pp. Life and labor on plantations run by the Society for the Propagation of the Gospel in Foreign Parts.

Breen, Henry H. St. Lucia: Historical, Statistical and Descriptive. London, 1844. 423 pp. Geography, commerce, and agricultural and economic history of the island.

Burn, William Laurence. Emancipation and Apprenticeship in the British West Indies. London, Jonathan Cape, 1937. 398 pp.

Burns, Alan Cuthbert. History of the British West Indies. London, Allen & Unwin, 1954. 821 pp. Comprehensive history of the islands through the nineteenth century; a predominantly narrative account, focusing on political, administrative, and military developments.

Caiger, Stephen L. British Honduras Past and Present. London, Allen & Unwin, 1954. 240 pp. General survey, primarily historical.

Carmichael, Mrs. A. C. Domestic Manners and Social Condition of the White, Coloured, and Negro Population of the West Indies. 2 vols. London, 1833. Descriptions of life in St. Vincent and Trinidad, 1821–26, by the wife of a planter.

Coleridge, Henry Nelson. Six Months in the West Indies in 1825. London, 1826. 328 pp. Observations on slaves and planters by the nephew of the Bishop of Barbados, who traveled with his uncle through the eastern Caribbean islands.

Craig, Hewan. The Legislative Council of Trinidad and Tobago. London, Faber & Faber, 1952. 195 pp. The history of the Council from 1831 to 1950, especially its development, composition, and the issues confronting it between 1925 and 1940, considered in the context of the changing structure of society in Trinidad.

Cumper, G. E. "Labour Demand and Supply in the Jamaican Sugar Industry, 1830–1950," *Social and Economic Studies*, II (No. 4, March, 1954), 37–86. A history of the Jamaican sugar industry from the emancipation of the slaves to the present, focusing on changes in the circumstances of and attitudes toward labor on the part of employers and workers.

——— "Population Movements in Jamaica, 1830–1950," *Social and Economic Studies*, V (1956), 261–80. The impact of emancipation and its aftermath on the sugar industry; the dispersal of estate laborers from the coastal lowlands to the interior hill country of Jamaica.

Curtin, Philip D. Two Jamaicas, 1830–1865: the Role of Ideas in a Tropical Colony. Cambridge, Harvard Univ. Press, 1955. 270 pp. The effects of the emancipation movement on culture and politics among the white, colored, and black sections of Jamaican society.

Davy, John. The West Indies, before and since Slave Emancipation, Comprising the Windward and Leeward Islands Military Command: Founded on Notes and Observations Collected during a Three Years' Residence. London, 1854. 551 pp. A detailed account focusing on nineteenth-century agriculture and economic conditions in the eastern Caribbean.

Edwards, Bryan. The History, Civil and Commercial, of the British Colonies in the West Indies. 2 vols. London, 1793. The classic eighteenth-century history of the islands; an invaluable picture of conditions after the American Revolution by a former planter, merchant, and political figure in Jamaica.

Froude, James Anthony. The English in the West Indies, or, The Bow of Ulysses. London, 1888. 373 pp. Observations, mainly gloomy, racially biased, and reactionary, on the social and economic conditions of the West Indian islands and on their political prospects, based on a visit by the renowned historian of England and her empire.

Goveia, Elsa V. A Study of the Historiography of the British West Indies to the End of the Nineteenth Century. Mexico D. F., Pan-American Institute of Geography and History, 1956. 183 pp. A comprehensive critical evalution of the most important colonial histories of all the islands.

———— "The West Indian Slave Laws of the Eighteenth Century," *Revista de Ciencias Sociales*, IV (1960), 75–106. The codes of law governing the behavior and punishment of slaves in the Spanish, French, and British plantations; emphasizes the basic similarities in content and enforcement, required for social stability under slavery.

Hall, Douglas. Free Jamaica: 1838–1865: an Economic History.

New Haven, Yale Univ. Press, 1959. 290 pp. The effects of emancipation—especially the substitution of wage for slave labor and the growth of small farming—and changes in tariff policies on Jamaican economy and politics.

Hamilton, Bruce. Barbados and the Confederation Question (1871–1885). London, Crown Agents for Overseas Governments & Administrations, 1956. xviii, 149 pp. Account of the conflict engendered by the efforts of the Colonial Office to federate Barbados with the Windward Islands.

Harlow, Vincent T. A History of Barbados 1625–1685. London, Oxford Univ. Press, 1926. 348 pp. Focuses on government, politics, and external trade.

Higham, C. S. S. The Development of the Leeward Islands under the Restoration, 1660–1688: a Study of the Foundations of the Old Colonial System. Cambridge, Cambridge Univ. Press, 1921. 266 pp. Deals with French-English rivalry, government, politics, the Caribs, the labor problem, and the growth of the sugar industry and its control by the Board of Trade.

Jefferys, Thomas. The West India Atlas . . . ; or, A Compendious Description of the West Indies. London, 1775. The earliest detailed and accurate set of West Indian maps. Contains large-scale charts of each of the islands and of many of their harbors.

Kingsley, Charles. At Last, a Christmas in the West Indies. New York, Macmillan, 1871. 334 pp. Solid and appreciative description of nature and life observed during a seven weeks' stay in Trinidad by a well-known novelist.

Le Page, R. B., and David de Camp. Jamaican Creole: an Historical Introduction to Jamaican Creole, and four Jamaican Creole Texts. London, Macmillan, 1960. 182 pp. An account of Jamaican settlement history and of the Old World origins of the population, notably of the slaves, in an endeavor to explain aspects of the local dialect; together with the text and translations of four stories, as told by an old Maroon from Accompong.

Lewis, Matthew Gregory. Journal of a West India Proprietor, ed. Mona Wilson. Boston, Houghton Mifflin, 1929. 356 pp. Perceptive account of two visits to Jamaica (1815 and 1817), by the

English heir to two sugar estates. The author was interested in Negro welfare and in exposing the evils of absentee landlordism.

Ligon, Richard. A True and Exact History of the Island of Barbados. London, 1657. 122 pp. Detailed account of all aspects of life in Barbados, notably of the growth of the sugar cane industry.

Long, Edward. The History of Jamaica, or, General Survey of the Antient and Modern State of that Island with Reflections on Its Situation, Settlements, Inhabitants, Climate, Products, Commerce, Laws and Government. 3 vols. London, 1774. Political, social, and economic history with a parish by parish survey of conditions in Jamaica on the eve of the American Revolution, and one of the most complete accounts of colonial government.

Lucas, Charles P. The West Indies, Vol. II of A Historical Geography of the British Colonies. Oxford, Clarendon Press, 1905. 348 pp. A systematic study of the discovery, settlement, and economic development of each of the islands.

Merrill, Gordon C. The Historical Geography of St. Kitts and Nevis, The West Indies. Mexico D. F., Pan-American Institute of Geography and History, 1958. 145 pp. The physical background, settlement, economic development, and patterns of estate and peasant agriculture, and their impacts on the landscapes of these two Leeward Islands.

Mintz, Sidney W. "Historical Sociology of the Jamaican Church-Founded Free Village System," *De West-Indische Gids,* XXXVIII (1958), 46–70. The rise of a peasantry in Jamaica at the time of emancipation and the social characteristics of the freedmen's villages founded by the Baptists and other denominations.

Newton, Arthur Percival. The European Nations in the West Indies 1493–1688. London, A. & C. Black Ltd., 1933. 357 pp. Repercussions of national policies and world events on all of the island empires.

Paget, Hugh. "The Free Village System in Jamaica," *Caribbean Quarterly,* I (No. 4, 1950), 7–19. The settlement of ex-slaves on the land in the decades following emancipation.

Pares, Richard. Merchants and Planters (*Economic History Review,* Supplement 4). Cambridge, Cambridge Univ. Press, 1960. 91

pp. Four essays on the West Indies in the seventeenth and eighteenth centuries: The Founders of Colonies; The Plantations; Colonial Trade; Debtors and Creditors.

———— A West-India Fortune. London, Longmans, Green, 1950. 374 pp. The history of the Pinneys' sugar plantation in Nevis and their sugar factor's business in Bristol, from the end of the seventeenth century to the mid-nineteenth century.

———— Yankees and Creoles: the Trade between North America and the West Indies before the American Revolution. New York, Longmans, Green, 1956. 168 pp. Account of the entrepreneurs, ships, cargoes, markets, and economic significance of the West India trade.

Parry, John H. "Plantation and Provision Ground," *Revista de historia de America*, No. 39 (June, 1955), pp. 1–20. The origin and spread of the crops grown by estates for export and by slaves (later by small farmers and tenants) for their own consumption and for local markets.

*————, and P. M. Sherlock. A Short History of the West Indies. London, Macmillan, 1956. 316 pp. Best general introduction to West Indian history from the discovery to 1954.

Pitman, Frank Wesley. The Development of the British West Indies 1700–1763. New Haven, Yale Univ. Press, 1917. 495 pp. Social and economic conditions, labor, trade, and commerce during the period of the sugar industry's greatest growth.

*Pope-Hennessy, James. West Indian Summer: a Retrospect. London, B. T. Batsford, 1943. 117 pp. Evocative retrospect combining the experiences of the author with those of nine other English visitors to the West Indies (Raleigh, Trollope, Froude, Waller, Coleridge, Mrs. Carmichael, Sloane, Kingsley, Dudley) from the fifteenth to the nineteenth centuries.

Ragatz, Lowell J. "Absentee Landlordism in the British Caribbean 1750–1833," *Agricultural History*, V (1931), 7–24. Shows the extent of nonresident plantation ownership, its causes, and its consequences, notably the decline of the white population and the deterioration of local governments.

———— The Fall of the Planter Class in the British Caribbean,

1763–1833: a Study in Social and Economic History. New York, Century, 1928. 520 pp. Pioneer study of the critical period from the height of West Indian opulence to the brink of ruin just before emancipation.

Roberts, G. W. "Emigration from the Island of Barbados," *Social and Economic Studies,* IV (1955), 245–88. The story of movement out of the most densely populated island between emancipation and the end of the First World War.

Rouse, Irving. "The West Indies: An Introduction," "The Arawak," and "The Carib," in Handbook of South American Indians, ed. Julian H. Steward, Vol. IV, pp. 495–565. Washington, Smithsonian Institution, 1948. The handbook comprises the seven-volume Bureau of American Ethnology Bulletin 143. The pages cited deal with the archeology, history, and ethnography of the American Indians of the islands.

Saul, S. B. "The British West Indies in Depression: 1880–1914," *Inter-American Economic Affairs,* XII (1958), 3–25. Survey of Britain's failure to help the sugar islands by trade and tariff manipulation during a period when the empire was generally prosperous; concentrates on Trinidad, Jamaica, Barbados, and British Guiana.

Schaw, Janet. Journal of a Lady of Quality, Being a Narrative of a Journey from Scotland to the West Indies, North Carolina, and Portugal, in the Years 1774 to 1776, ed. E. W. Andrews and C. M. Andrews. New Haven, Yale Univ. Press, 1923. 341 pp. Life and landscape in Antigua and St. Kitts, as seen by a young lady from Scotland.

Schomburgk, Robert Hermann. The History of Barbados, Comprising a Geographical and Statistical Description of the Island; a Sketch of Historical Events since the Settlement; and an Account of Its Geology and Natural Productions. London, 1848. 722 pp. Encyclopaedic work by an able scholar.

Sewell, William Grant. The Ordeal of Free Labour in the West Indies. New York, 1861. 325 pp. The impact of emancipation in each of the islands.

Shephard, Cecil Y. "Peasant Agriculture in the Leeward and Windward Islands, Part I: The Development of Peasant Agriculture," *Tropical Agriculture*, XXIV (1947), 61–71. Historical survey of the development of various types of land tenure: laborers' provision grounds, share cropping, cash tenancy, squatting, and freehold tenure.

Shephard, Charles. An Historical Account of the Island of Saint Vincent. London, 1831. Good account of the Carib war of 1795, and of contemporary conditions in the island.

Sloane, Hans. A Voyage to the Islands Madera, Barbados, Nieves, S. Christophers and Jamaica, with the Natural History of the Herbs and Trees, Four-footed Beasts, Fishes, Birds, Insects, Reptiles, &c of the Last of Those Islands. 2 vols. London, 1707, 1725. Comprehensive and fascinating survey, principally of Jamaica, by a physician and naturalist who lived there from 1687 to 1689.

Smith, M. G. "Social Structure in the British Caribbean about 1820," *Social and Economic Studies*, I (No. 4, August, 1953), 55–80. A functional analysis of West Indian society before emancipation, utilizing contemporary accounts from Jamaica and St. Vincent.

Smith, William. The Natural History of Nevis and the Rest of the English Leeward Charibbee Islands in America. Cambridge, England, 1745. Description in the form of letters from a local rector.

Starkey, Otis P. The Economic Geography of Barbados: a Study of the Relationships between Environmental Variations and Economic Development. New York, Columbia Univ. Press, 1939. 228 pp. Development of the sugar economy and of production and consumption patterns from the seventeenth to the twentieth century.

Sturge, Joseph, and Thomas Harvey. The West Indies in 1837, Being the Journal of a Visit to Antigua, Montserrat, Dominica, St. Lucia, Barbados, and Jamaica, Undertaken for the Purpose of Ascertaining the Actual Condition of the Negro Population of Those Islands. London, 1838. 380 pp. Description by two anti-slavery leaders of social and economic conditions during the apprenticeship period immediately after emancipation.

Thornton, A. P. West-India Policy under the Restoration. Oxford, Clarendon Press, 1956. 280 pp. Relations between the English crown and its West Indian possessions during the heyday of the sugar economy in the latter part of the seventeenth century.

Trollope, Anthony. The West Indies and the Spanish Main. London, 1860. 395 pp. Witty and perceptive account of a sojourn in the islands, especially in Jamaica, by the famous novelist.

Verteuil, L. A. A. de. Trinidad: Its Geography, Natural Resources, Administration, Present Condition, and Prospects. London, 1858. 508 pp. A useful compendium by a local official; essentially a description of the island in the mid-nineteenth century. Second edition (1884) contains historical account.

Waller, John Augustine. A Voyage in the West Indies, Containing Various Observations Made during a Residence in Barbados and Several of the Leeward Islands. London, 1820. 104 pp. A naval surgeon's picture of island society, notably in Barbados, and of slave trade on the eve of its formal abolition by Great Britain.

Williams, Eric. Capitalism and Slavery. Chapel Hill, Univ. of North Carolina Press, 1944. 285 pp. A study of the role of the slave trade and of West Indian slavery in the growth of the plantation system in particular and of British economic and industrial organization in general, and of the part played by self-interest in determining the diverse and shifting attitudes toward slavery on the part of planters, officials, humanitarians, and industrialists.

Williamson, James A. The Caribbee Islands under the Proprietory Patents. London, Oxford Univ. Press, 1926. 234 pp. Politics and government in the Lesser Antilles up to 1660.

Wrong, Humphrey Hume. Government of the West Indies. Oxford, Clarendon Press, 1923. 190 pp. Surveys West Indian governments and politics from the first British settlements up to 1922.

4. CONTEMPORARY AFFAIRS

Abrahams, Peter. Jamaica, an Island Mosaic. London, H.M.S.O., 1957. 283 pp. General description with historical background, social and political commentary, and landscape vignettes.

"Agricultural Marketing—a West Indies Problem," *West Indian Economist,* II (No. 6, December, 1959), 19–24. Analysis of the difficulties involved in internal and external marketing of West Indian agricultural products.

Augelli, John P. "The British Virgin Islands: a West Indian Anomaly," *Geographical Review,* LXIV (1956), 43–58. Survey of the economy of these islands, focusing on their relationships with the American Virgin Islands.

————, and Harry W. Taylor. "Race and Population Patterns in Trinidad," *Annals of the Association of American Geographers,* L (1960), 123–38. Discussion of the distribution of Negroes and East Indians in terms of principal land use patterns and occupational roles.

Banton, Michael. White and Coloured: the Behaviour of British People towards Coloured Immigrants. London, Jonathan Cape, 1959. 218 pp. How West Indians and others are regarded and treated, and how they react, in several interracial contexts in England: at coastal dockyards, in universities, and in industrial cities.

"Barbados—Present and Future," *West Indian Economist,* III (No. 1, July, 1960), 15–21. Assessment of the character and potentiality of the Barbadian economy.

Beckwith, Martha Warren. Black Roadways: a Study of Jamaican Folk Life. Chapel Hill, North Carolina, Univ. of North Carolina Press, 1929. 243 pp. General picture of peasant life and thought in rural Jamaica.

Bethel, Jeanette. "A National Accounts Study of the Economy of Barbados," *Social and Economic Studies,* IX (1960), 123–252. Economic characteristics, recent development, and the contributions made by the various sectors of the economy, statistically considered.

Blanshard, Paul. Democracy and Empire in the Caribbean: a Contemporary Review. . . . New York, Macmillan, 1947. 379 pp. Social and political problems of each of the territories during the years 1942–46.

Blaut, J., R. Blaut, N. Harman, and M. H. Moerman. "A Study of the Cultural Determinants of Soil Erosion and Conservation in the Blue Mountains of Jamaica," *Social and Economic Studies*, VIII (1959), 403–20. The ways in which peasant farmers view their situation and resources, and how these attitudes affect their treatment of the land.

Bradley, Paul. "Mass Parties in Jamaica: Structure and Organization," *Social and Economic Studies*, IX (1960), in press. A study of the two major political parties of Jamaica, Bustamente's Jamaica Labour Party and Manley's People's National Party.

Braithwaite, Lloyd. "The Development of Higher Education in the West Indies," *Social and Economic Studies*, VII (1958), 1–64. A chronicle and assessment of efforts to establish colleges and universities in the islands, the types of training envisaged by the promoters, and the relations between these schemes and the social structure of the area.

*———— "Social Stratification in Trinidad," *Social and Economic Studies*, II (Nos. 2 and 3, October, 1953), 5–175. Detailed analysis of class, race, and culture in Trinidad, historically and sociologically considered.

———— "Sociology and Demographic Research in the Caribbean," *Social and Economic Studies*, VI (1957), 523–71. Critical survey of current work in West Indian census and population analysis, especially of studies bearing on fertility and migration.

British Honduras (British Information Services, Reference Division, I.D. 1319). January, 1959. 26 pp. General description of the territory and its people, with economic, social, and constitutional data.

"Canada-West Indies Economic and Political Relations," *West Indian Economist*, I (No. 6, December, 1958), 15–23. The history, contemporary patterns and problems, and possible future of trade and other contacts between the islands and the North American dominion.

*Clarke, Edith. My Mother Who Fathered Me, a Study of the Family in Three Selected Communities in Jamaica. London, Allen & Unwin, 1957. 216 pp. Anthropological study of the functional roles of patterns of land tenure, household organization, mating, kinship, and economy.

Cohen, Yehudi. "Character Formation and Social Structure in a

Jamaican Community," *Psychiatry*, XVIII (1955), 275–96. The life cycles, relationships, demands, and expectations of individuals in a small mountain area, in whom the author observed deep-seated hostilities rarely given direct expression.

Collins, Sydney. Coloured Minorities in Britain: Studies in British Race Relations Based on African, West Indian, and Asiatic Immigrants. London, Lutterworth Press, 1957. 258 pp. Descriptions of West Indian and other non-European communities of varying social circumstances in Wales, Tyneside, and Lancashire.

Collymore, Frank A. Notes for a Glossary of Words and Phrases of Barbadian Dialect. Bridgetown, Barbados, Advocate Co., 1955. 77 pp. The uses and sources of elements in a distinctive West Indian patois, and their links with Elizabethan and modern Standard English.

Crowley, D. J. "Plural and Differential Acculturation in Trinidad," *American Anthropologist*, LIX (1957), 817–24. Presents the view that Negroes, East Indians, Chinese, Europeans, and others in "one of the most cosmopolitan places on earth" have become "Creolized" and share a basic culture in common.

Cumper, G. E. "Employment in Barbados," *Social and Economic Studies*, VIII (1959), 105–46. History of the labor market, present-day employment problems, the impact of emigration, and the prospects for employment in the major sectors of the economy.

——— "The Jamaican Family: Village and Estate," *Social and Economic Studies*, VII (1958), 76–108. A discussion of economic problems, especially agricultural employment and productivity, as related to environment and to population and family structure in three different Jamaican areas.

——— "A Modern Jamaican Sugar Estate," *Social and Economic Studies*, III (1954), 119–60. The evolution of settlement and production patterns on Frome, one of the largest Jamaican plantations.

——— The Social Structure of the British Caribbean (Excluding Jamaica). 3 parts. Kingston, Jamaica, Extra-Mural Department, University College of the West Indies, 1949. Detailed comparative analyses of demography, land use and tenure, occupations, and race, based on the 1946 census.

*———, ed. The Economy of The West Indies. Kingston, Jamaica, Institute of Social and Economic Research, University College of the West Indies, 1960. 273 pp. The first book-length survey of the West Indian economy, comprising the following chapters: G. E. Cumper, "The Development of the West Indies"; G. W. Roberts, "Movements in Population and the Labour Force"; David Lowenthal, "Physical Resources"; C. O'Loughlin and L. Best, "Economic Structure in the West Indies"; G. E. Cumper, "Employment and Unemployment in the West Indies," "Personal Consumption in the West Indies"; A. R. Prest, "Public Finance"; E. F. Nash, "Trading Problems of the British West Indies"; A. D. Knox, "Trade and Customs Union in the West Indies."

Development towards Self-Government in the Caribbean: a Symposium Held under the Auspices of the Netherlands Universities Foundation for International Co-operation. The Hague, W. van Hoeve, 1955. 285 pp. Includes the following on the British Caribbean, as well as many papers on French, Dutch, and American territories: E. W. Evans, "A Survey of the Present Constitutional Situation in the British West Indies"; Colin A. Hughes, "A Sociological Analysis of the Political Situation in the British West Indies"; C. M. MacInnes, "Constitutional Development of the British West Indies," "British Caribbean Federation," "Development and Welfare in the British West Indies."

Doran, Edwin, Jr. "The Caicos Conch Trade," *Geographical Review,* XLVIII (1958) 388–401. The history, distribution, and technology of the principal cash crop of the inhabitants of the Turks and Caicos Islands, and its ecological and commercial significance in the Caribbean.

"The Economics of Development in The West Indies," *West Indian Economist,* I (No. 11, May, 1959), 13–20. Agriculture, labor, public works, trade and shipping, and monetary problems, in the light of a 1957 conference on economic development at the University College of the West Indies.

"The Economies of the Small Islands," *West Indian Economist,* II

(No. 4, October, 1959), 15–22. Assessment of each of the Windward and Leeward territories, principally in terms of how well they have succeeded in maintaining a viable agricultural economy, like that of Barbados; prospects for major industrial or commercial development, as in Jamaica and Trinidad, are considered remote.

"The Economy of Trinidad," *West Indian Economist,* II (No. 9, March, 1960), 14–20. A study of the sectors contributing to the economy of Trinidad, compared with the Jamaican economy.

Edwards, David T. "An Economic Study of Agriculture in the Yallahs Valley Area of Jamaica," *Social and Economic Studies,* III (1954), 316–41. The geography, farm organization, land use, productivity, income, and employment situation of a densely populated hill area near Kingston, where attack against poverty and soil erosion began with the establishment in 1951 of Jamaica's first local Land Authority.

——— Report on an Economic Study of Small Farming in Jamaica. Kingston, Jamaica, University College of the West Indies, Institute of Social and Economic Research, in press. About 368 pp. Land use and tenure, labor, expenditures, and incomes among farm households in representative ecological situations throughout Jamaica.

Engledow, Frank L. Report on Agriculture, Fisheries, Forestry and Veterinary Matters (West India Royal Commission, Cmd. 6608). London, H.M.S.O., 1945. 235 pp. Survey of agricultural processing and marketing, land use and tenure, soil exhaustion and erosion, and the special problems of each territory. Made in connection with the West India Royal Commission (1938–39).

The Federal Principle, *Caribbean Quarterly,* VI (Nos. 2 & 3, May, 1960), 67–239. A series of lectures given in Port of Spain, Trinidad, 1959, with a foreword by the governor-general of The West Indies. Includes the following: C. V. Gocking, "Early Constitutional History of Jamaica"; R. N. Murray, "The Road Back— Jamaica after 1866"; Bruce Procope, "The Temporary Federal Mace"; H. O. B. Wooding, "The Constitutional History of Trinidad and Tobago"; Coleridge Harris, "The Constitutional History of the Windwards"; Cecil A. Kelsick, "The Constitutional History of the Leewards"; S. S. Ramphal, "Federalism in the West Indies"; "A Summary of Constitutional Advances: Trinidad and Tobago" (Harvey de Costa), "Jamaica" (Harvey de Costa), "The Leeward and Windward Islands" (F. A. Phillips).

*Federation of the West Indies, Special number of *Social and Economic Studies,* VI (No. 2, June, 1957), 99–328. Includes the following papers: Paul Knaplund, "Introduction"; Ronald V. Sires, "Government in the B.W.I.: An Outline"; Lloyd Braithwaite, "Progress towards Federation"; David Lowenthal, "Two Federations"; Dudley Seers, "Economic and Financial Aspects"; Gordon K. Lewis, "Constitutional Aspects"; Morley Ayearst, "Political Aspects"; G. W. Roberts, "Some Demographic Considerations"; Lloyd Braithwaite, " 'Federal' Associations in the B.W.I."

*Fermor, Patrick Leigh. The Traveller's Tree: a Journey through the Caribbean Islands. New York, Harper, 1950. 403 pp. Best modern travel account; perceptive and beautifully written sketches of history, landscape, architecture, and the contemporary scene. The author visited, in addition to Martinique, Guadelope, and Haiti, all the British territories except St. Vincent and Montserrat.

"The Future of Jamaica's Sugar Industry," *West Indian Economist,* II (No. 8, February, 1960), 17–23. Study of a government report on the causes of a recent sugar estate strike, and of industry finances and production costs.

Great Britain. Colonial Office. An Economic Survey of the Colonial Territories 1951. Vol. IV: The West Indian and American Territories (Colonial No. 281–4). London, H.M.S.O., 1953. 274 pp. Island by island data for production and trade, now somewhat out of date but still the most comprehensive one-volume survey.

Hadley, C. V. D. "Personality Patterns, Social Class, and Aggression in the British West Indies," *Human Relations,* II (1949), 349–62. Historical and psychological explanations of patterns of behavior categorized as proletarian, lower-middle-class, and upper-middle-class.

Henriques, Fernando. Family and Colour in Jamaica. London, Eyre & Spottiswoode, 1953. 196 pp. A study of the interplay of color prejudice and family structure and values, primarily among upper-middle-class Jamaicans.

Herskovits, Melville J., and Frances S. Herskovits. Trinidad Village. New York, Knopf, 1947. 351 pp. Pioneer anthropological study of culture and society in a small community in northeastern Trinidad, emphasizing the retention of African customs—notably in religion—and showing how these have been reshaped to fit preponderantly European ways of life.

Katzin, Margaret Fisher. "The Business of Higglering in Jamaica," *Social and Economic Studies,* IX (1960), 297–331. A description of the internal distribution by which produce grown on small farms for sale locally is bought and transported by middlemen (mainly women) to city markets; the expenses and profits of various types of higglers; and the efficiency of the system relative to other potential methods of marketing produce in Jamaica.

—————— "The Jamaican Country Higgler," *Social and Economic Studies,* VIII (1959), 421–35. An account of the weekly routine of a typical higgler—one of the thousands of women who buy produce in rural areas, carry it to city markets, and sell it, thus linking the isolated small farmer and the consumer.

Kerr, Madeline. Personality and Conflict in Jamaica. Liverpool, Liverpool Univ. Press, 1952. 221 pp. The social and cultural background, daily life, and psychological problems of rural Jamaicans.

Klass, Morton. East Indians in Trinidad: a Study of Cultural Persistence. New York, Columbia Univ. Press, in press.

Kuczynski, R. R. A Demographic Survey of the British Colonial Empire. Vol. III: The West Indian and American Territories (Royal Institute of International Affairs). London, Oxford Univ. Press, 1953. 497 pp. Analysis of population statistics for each of the territories; comparisons of birth and death figures with census estimates.

"Labour and Management in The West Indies," *West Indian Economist,* II (No. 10, April, 1960), 14–21. Analysis of trade unionism in all the islands and of the attitudes and actions of workers and employers.

Laird, Colin. "Trinidad Town House, or, The Rise and Decline of a Domestic Architecture," *Caribbean Quarterly*, III (1954), 188–98. An illustrated study of the "Carpenters' Gothic" dwellings characteristic of Port of Spain, Trinidad.

Le Page, Robert B. "General Outlines of Creole English Dialects in the British Caribbean," *Orbis* (Louvain), VI (1957), 373–91; VII (1958), 54–64. A study of the background, phonology, grammar, and vocabulary of Jamaican and other West Indian variant forms of English.

Lewis, W. Arthur. "The Industrialization of the British West Indies," *Caribbean Economic Review*, II (No. 1, May, 1950), 1–61. Survey of the need for industrialization, of the industries best suited to the available resources and markets of the area, and of the appropriate techniques and policies for establishing them.

Lind, Andrew W. "Adjustment Patterns among the Jamaican Chinese," *Social and Economic Studies*, VII (1958), 143–64. The history of Chinese immigration in Jamaica, the economic roles of the Chinese, and relations between the Chinese community and other Jamaicans.

Lowenthal, David. "The Population of Barbados," *Social and Economic Studies*, VI (1957), 445–501. Analysis of the causes and consequences of population pressure in Barbados, viewed in historical, ecological, social, and political perspective; comparisons with other British Caribbean territories; survey of resource potentials.

——— "The West Indies Chooses a Capital," *Geographical Review*, XLIV (1958), 336–64. Images and stereotypes of island character, especially of Barbados, Jamaica, and Trinidad, as reflected in the competition for the federal capital site; the geographical ideals and realities of semi-autonomous insular units.

Macmillan, Mona. The Land of Look Behind: a Study of Jamaica. London, Faber and Faber, 1957. 224 pp. General account focusing on the contemporary social and economic scene.

Macmillan, William Miller. Warning from the West Indies: a Tract for the Empire. 2d ed. Harmondsworth, Penguin Books, 1938. 184 pp. The character and causes of the social and economic unrest in the islands that resulted in the disturbances of 1937 and the appointment of the West India Royal Commission in 1938.

McMorris, C. S. Small-Farm Financing in Jamaica. Supplement to *Social and Economic Studies,* Vol. 6, No. 3, 1957. 128 pp. Aspects of the economics of peasant farming.

Maunder, W. F. Employment in an Underdeveloped Area: a Sample Survey of Kingston, Jamaica (Yale Caribbean Series No. 3). New Haven, Yale Univ. Press, 1960. 215 pp. Statistical study of the components and availability of the labor force, with special reference to poverty and unemployment.

Mittelholzer, Edgar. With a Carib Eye. London, Secker & Warburg, 1958. 192 pp. Essays and travel sketches about several of the British West Indies by a British Guianese novelist.

Moser, C. A. The Measurement of Levels of Living with Special Reference to Jamaica (Colonial Research Studies No. 24). London, H.M.S.O., 1957. 106 pp. Evaluation of Jamaican statistics and other data in the fields of education, nutrition, health, and housing.

O'Loughlin, Carleen. "The Economies of Montserrat, Antigua, and St. Kitts-Nevis," *Social and Economic Studies,* VIII (1959), 147–78; 229–64; 377–402. Three national accounts studies showing patterns of earnings and expenditure in the Leeward Islands.

Paget, E. "Land-Use and Settlement in Jamaica," in Geographical Essays on British Tropical Lands, ed. R. W. Steel and C. A. Fisher, pp. 181–223. London, George Philip & Son, 1956. Present patterns of land use and settlement and their physical and historical backgrounds.

"The Pattern of West Indies Trade Relations," *West Indian Economist,* II (No. 2, August, 1959), 20–26. Analysis of West Indian export and import sources and destinations, both by commodity group and by territory as well as for the federation as a whole; survey of the extent and types of inter-island trade; and discussion of the implications in terms of customs union.

Pearse, Andrew C. "Education in the British Caribbean: Social and

Economic Background," *Vox Guyanae* (Paramaribo, Surinam), II (1956), 9–24. An account of schools, teachers, and students in the West Indies from the eighteenth century to the present; a study of the relations between social motivations and systems of instruction, and of the problems involved in developing suitable forms of education.

Pope-Hennessey, James. The Baths of Absalom: a Footnote to Froude. London, Allan Wingate, 1954. 64 pp. Critique of British administration in the smaller islands, contrasting what the author views as the apathy, squalor, and stagnation of Dominica and St. Lucia with conditions in French Martinique.

Proctor, Jesse H., Jr. "Britain's Pro-Federation Policy in the Caribbean: an Inquiry into Motivation," *Canadian Journal of Economics and Political Science*, XXII (1956), 319–31. Analysis of the reasons for Britain's support of West Indian federation, and the rationale behind her policy statements and recommendations.

Proudfoot, Mary. Britain and the United States in the Caribbean: a Comparative Study in Methods of Development. London, Faber & Faber, 1954. 434 pp. Constitutional relationships and ways of dealing with specific economic, social, and political problems in Jamaica, Trinidad, Barbados, and St. Lucia, compared with Puerto Rico and the American Virgin Islands.

"Report on the University College," *West Indian Economist*, I (No. 9, March, 1959), 15–21. The recommendations made by a committee under the chairmanship of A. S. Cato, which reviewed the policy and state of affairs at the University College of the West Indies in 1957–58: notably the problem of expanding to include engineering and agriculture; the question of affiliation with the University of London; and the role of the Extra-Mural Department.

Roberts, George W. The Population of Jamaica: an Analysis of Its Structure and Growth. London, Cambridge Univ. Press, 1957. 356 pp. Comprehensive study of all aspects of demography in the island.

——— "Some Aspects of Mating and Fertility in the West Indies," *Population Studies*, VIII (1955), 199–227. Study of ways in which birth rates and fertility in several West Indian territories vary with sex ratios (number of men compared with women of child-bearing age) and with family forms.

Roberts, George W., and D. O. Mills. Study of External Migration Affecting Jamaica: 1953–1955. Supplement to Vol. VII (No. 2, 1958) of *Social and Economic Studies*. 126 pp. The extent and character of Jamaican migration to the United Kingdom, and its effects on the economy and labor force, notably the sugar industry.

Rubin, Vera, ed. Caribbean Studies: a Symposium. Jamaica, Institute of Social and Economic Research, 1957. 124 pp. 2d ed., Seattle, Washington, Univ. of Washington Press, 1960. Includes the following papers, presented at a meeting of the American Association for the Advancement of Science: Charles Wagley, "Plantation America: a Culture Sphere"; Preston E. James, "Man-Land Relations in the Caribbean Area"; Elena Padilla, "Contemporary Rural-Social Types in the Caribbean Area"; M. G. Smith, "The African Heritage in the Caribbean"; Eric Williams, "Race Relations in Caribbean Society"; Raymond T. Smith, "The Family in the Caribbean"; Robert A. Manners, "Methods of Community-Analysis in the Caribbean"; Lloyd Braithwaite, "The Present Status of the Social Sciences in the Caribbean"; Vera Rubin, "Cultural Perspectives in Caribbean Research."

Ruck, S. K., ed. The West Indian Comes to Britain: a Report Prepared for the London Parochial Charities by the Family Welfare Association. London, Routledge & Kegan Paul, 1960. 187 pp. Includes chapters by Douglas Manley on the West Indian background and the history and effects of migration since 1900, by Ivor de Souza on the arrival and reception of migrants in England, and by John Hyndman on the life of the West Indian in London.

Seaga, E. P. G. "Parent-Teacher Relationships in a Jamaican Village," *Social and Economic Studies*, IV (1955), 289–302. Attitudes of parents and teachers toward education in general, toward the local elementary school, and toward each other.

Senior, Clarence, and Douglas Manley. A Report on Jamaican Migration to Great Britain. Kingston, Jamaica, Government Printer, 1955. 67 pp. The character of the migration from Jamaica to England and an analysis of its actual and potential effects on the Jamaican local economy.

Sherlock, Philip M. West Indian Story. London, Longmans, Green, 1960. 134 pp. Description of the settlement of different peoples in the West Indies, incorporating contemporary descriptions.

Simey, Thomas Spensley. Welfare and Planning in the West Indies. Oxford, Clarendon Press, 1946. 267 pp. A sophisticated survey of West Indian society and of the measures taken to deal with social problems up to the close of the Second World War.

Simpson, George Eaton. "Jamaican Revivalist Cults," *Social and Economic Studies,* V (No. 4, December, 1956), 321–442. An account of lower-class religious organization, beliefs, and revivalist cults in West Kingston, Jamaica.

Smith, M. G. "Dark Puritan: the Life and Work of Norman Paul," *Caribbean Quarterly,* V (1957–58), 34–47; 85–98; VI (1960), 48–59. Installments of the life story of a Grenadian preacher.

———— "Education and Occupational Choice in Rural Jamaica," *Social and Economic Studies,* IX (1960), 332–54. A study of the ambitions and goals of young men in several areas, revealing "a formidable gap between reality and desire."

*———— A Framework for Caribbean Studies (Caribbean Affairs Series). Mona, Jamaica, Extra-Mural Department, University College of the West Indies, 1955. 70 pp. Critical review of various approaches to the study of West Indian society and culture: Afro-American research, the folk-urban continuum, psychological studies and interpretations, social stratification and differentiation, color and ethnic background; presentation of an analytical model combining several of these within the framework of social pluralism.

———— A Report on Labour Supply in Rural Jamaica. Kingston, Jamaica, Government Printer, 1956. 167 pp. Inquiry into problems of work and employment, based on a comparative analysis of four areas where employers complained of labor shortages and four areas where the supply of labor was considered adequate.

———— "The Transformation of Land Rights by Transmission in Carriacou," *Social and Economic Studies,* V (1956), 103–38.

Study of relationships between kinship and legal and actual systems of land tenure in an island in the Grenadines.

Smith, M. G., Roy Augier, and Rex Nettleford. The Ras Tafari Movement in Kingston, Jamaica. Kingston, Jamaica, University College of the West Indies, 1960. 54 pp. The ideological and socio-economic background of a group involved in serious disturbances in 1960, and the beliefs and goals of its adherents.

————, and G. J. Kruijer. A Sociological Manual for Extension Workers in the Caribbean (Caribbean Affairs Series). Kingston, Jamaica, The Extra-Mural Department, University College of the West Indies, 1957. 255 pp. Aspects of Jamaican social life and economy, from housing and nutrition to settlement patterns and social stratification.

Smith, Raymond T. The Negro Family in British Guiana: Family, Structure, and Social Status in the Villages. London, Routledge & Kegan Paul, 1956. 282 pp. The history, economy, and social organization of three coastal villages established by ex-slaves in the mid-nineteenth century, and the relation of rural family patterns and status systems to Guianese society as a whole.

*Social and Cultural Pluralism in the Caribbean (Annals of the New York Academy of Sciences, LXXXIII [1960], 761–916). Includes the following papers on social, cultural, political, and racial aspects of class and community structure and functions in the West Indies, notably the British Caribbean: M. G. Smith, "Social and Cultural Pluralism"; David Lowenthal, "The Range and Variation of Caribbean Societies"; Lambros Comitas, "Metropolitan Influences in the Caribbean: The West Indies"; Lloyd Braithwaite, "Social Stratification and Cultural Pluralism"; Daniel J. Crowley, "Cultural Assimilation in a Multiracial Society"; Morton Klass, "East and West Indian: Cultural Complexity in Trinidad"; Wendell Bell, "Attitudes of Jamaican Elites toward The West Indies Federation"; Leonard Broom, "Urbanization and the Plural Society"; Wilfred G. O. Cartey, "The Writer in the Caribbean"; Elliott P. Skinner, "Group Dynamics and Social Stratification in British Guiana."

Straw, K. H. "Some Preliminary Results of a Survey of Income and

Consumption Patterns in a Sample of Households in Barbados," *Social and Economic Studies*, I (No. 4, August, 1953), 5–40. Shows how income and expenditure on food and other items vary seasonally with the sugar crop.

"A Study of the Growth of Three West Indian Economies," *West Indian Economist*, I (No. 12, June, 1959), 14–20. Comparative study of Jamaica, Trinidad, and British Guiana economies and income patterns.

Swan, Michael. British Guiana: the Land of Six Peoples. London, H.M.S.O., 1957. 235 pp. Informative travel diary with sketches of the local history, literature, personalities, and social, economic, and political problems of the South American territory.

———— The Marches of El Dorado: British Guiana, Brazil, Venezuela. Boston, Beacon Press, 1958. 304 pp. Perceptive account of the peoples and landscapes of the sparsely inhabited interior of British Guiana.

"Symposium on the Report of the Trade and Tariffs Commission," *Social and Economic Studies*, IX (1960), 1–40. Critiques by four economists of the 1958 reports on federal customs union.

Taylor, Douglas. "The Caribs of Dominica" (Anthropological Papers, No. 3), in *Bulletin, Bureau of American Ethnology*, No. 119 (1938), 103–59. The social, domestic, and economic life of the only remaining indigenous American Indians in the West Indies.

Thorne, Alfred P. Size, Structure and Growth of the Economy of Jamaica. Supplement to *Social and Economic Studies*, IV (No. 4, 1955). 112 pp. A national economic accounts study.

"The Tourist Dollar and Jamaica's Economy," *West Indian Economist*, II (No. 1, July, 1959), 15–21. Discussion of the present impact and future prospects of what is in Jamaica, and is likely to become for the federation, a mainstay of the economy.

Trinidad Carnival Issue. *Caribbean Quarterly*, IV (Nos. 3 and 4, March and June, 1956). 318 pp. Description, historical background, and social implications of the most popular and colorful annual festival in the West Indies. Includes the following papers: Andrew Pearse, "Carnival in Nineteenth Century Trinidad"; Daniel J. Crowley, "The Traditional Masques of Carnival"; Bar-

bara E. Powrie, "The Changing Attitude of the Coloured Middle Class Towards Carnival"; Andrew Pearse, ed., "Mitto Sampson on Calypso Legends of the Nineteenth Century"; Daniel J. Crowley, "The Midnight Robbers"; Bruce Procope, "The Dragon Band or Devil Band"; Andrew T. Carr, "Pierrot Grenada."

"The West Indies: New Bottle, Old Wine," *Population Bulletin*, XIV (1958), 17–34. General survey of population growth, migration, and prospects for birth control.

Whitson, Agnes M., and Lucy Frances Horsfall. Britain and the West Indies. London, Longmans, Green, 1948. 87 pp. Attractive illustrated summary of West Indian history, government, economy, and society.

Williams, Eric. Federation: Two Public Lectures. Port of Spain, Trinidad, People's National Movement, 1956. 60 pp. Early statements favoring federation by the future premier of Trinidad and Tobago.

5. BELLES-LETTRES

Allfrey, Phyllis Shand. The Orchid House. London, Constable, 1953. 235 pp. A novel about a family in Dominica.

Anthology of West Indian Poetry (*Caribbean Quarterly*, Federation Commemoration Issue, Vol. V, No. 3, April, 1958). Trinidad, Gov. Print. Off., 1958. 226 pp. Poems by thirty-eight West Indians.

Black, Clinton. Tales of Old Jamaica. Kingston, Jamaica, Pioneer Press, 1952. 121 pp.

Hearne, John. The Autumn Equinox. London, Faber and Faber, 1959. 272 pp. This and the three following titles by Hearne are novels set in Jamaica.

―――― The Faces of Love. London, Faber and Faber, 1957. 267 pp.

―――― Stranger at the Gate. London, Faber and Faber, 1955. 304 pp.

―――― Voices under the Window. London, Faber and Faber, 1956. 163 pp.

°Lamming, George. In the Castle of My Skin. London, M. Joseph, 1953. 303 pp. A novel of childhood in Barbados.

—————— Of Age and Innocence. London, M. Joseph, 1958. 413 pp. A novel set in a mythical West Indian island.

Mais, Roger. Black Lightning. London, Jonathan Cape, 1955. 222 pp. This and the two following titles by Mais are novels with Jamaican settings.

—————— Brother Man. London, Jonathan Cape, 1954. 191 pp.

—————— The Hills Were Joyful Together. London, Jonathan Cape, 1953. 288 pp.

Manley, Edna, ed. Focus: An Anthology of Contemporary Jamaican Writings. Kingston, Jamaica, Extra-Mural Department, University College of the West Indies, 1956. 243 pp. Short stories, poems, and plays.

Mittelholzer, Edgar. The Adding Machine: a Fable for Capitalists and Commercialists. Kingston, Jamaica, Pioneer Press, 1954. 102 pp. A parable with a West Indian island setting.

—————— The Life and Death of Sylvia. London, Secker & Warburg, 1953. 288 pp. A novel about middle-class life in British Guiana.

*—————— A Morning at the Office. London, Hogarth Press, 1950. 246 pp. A novel about people of all classes in Port of Spain, Trinidad.

—————— Of Trees and the Sea. London, Secker & Warburg, 1956. 256 pp. A novel set in Barbados.

—————— The Weather Family. London, Secker & Warburg, 1958. 339 pp. A novel set in Barbados.

Naipaul, V. S. Miguel Street. London, Andre Deutsch, 1959. 222 pp. Sketches about characters in a neighborhood in Port of Spain, Trinidad.

—————— The Mystic Masseur. London, Andre Deutsch, 1957. 215 pp. A satirical novel about the rising fortunes of an East Indian in Trinidad.

—————— The Suffrage of Elvira. London, Andre Deutsch, 1958. 240 pp. A novel about an election in a rural village in Trinidad.

Reid, Victor Stafford. New Day. New York, Alfred A. Knopf, 1949. 374 pp. A historical novel about Jamaica.

—————, et al. 14 Jamaican Short Stories. Kingston, Jamaica, The Pioneer Press, 1950. 135 pp.

Salkey, Andrew. A Quality of Violence. London, Hutchinson, 1959.

205 pp. A novel about life on the north coast of Jamaica early in the twentieth century.

————, ed. West Indian Stories. London, Faber & Faber, 1960. An anthology of stories by West Indian authors selected by a West Indian novelist.

Selvon, Samuel. A Brighter Sun. London, Allan Wingate, 1952. 236 pp. A novel about a young East Indian couple in Trinidad.

———— An Island Is a World. London, Allan Wingate, 1955. 288 pp. A novel set in Trinidad.

———— Turn Again Tiger. London, MacGibbon & Kee, 1958. 219 pp. A novel about East Indians in rural Trinidad; sequel to *A Brighter Sun.*

———— Ways of Sunlight. London, MacGibbon & Kee, 1957. 188 pp. Short stories set in Trinidad and London.

Seymour, A. J., ed. Anthology of West Indian Poetry (*Kykoveral* No. 22). Georgetown, British Guiana, 1957. 99 pp. Poems by twenty-eight authors.

Waugh, Alec. Island in the Sun: a Story of the 1950's Set in the West Indies. New York, Farrar, Straus and Cudahy, 1955. 538 pp.

6. PERIODICALS AND NEWSPAPERS

Barbados Advocate (Bridgetown, Barbados), 1895–   . Barbados' only daily newspaper; six days a week.

Bim (Bridgetown, Barbados), 1952–   . Appears about twice a year. Literary periodical, publishing short stories, poems, travel articles, and criticism.

Caribbean (Port of Spain, Trinidad), 1947–60. Monthly. Information bulletin of the Caribbean Commission; regional news items and short articles on tourism, resource development, and many other subjects of general or local interest. Ceased publication in 1960.

Caribbean Economic Review (Port of Spain, Trinidad), 1949–54. Half-yearly until 1951; then annually, until publication ceased after 1954. Papers concerned with agriculture, industry, trade, and population, for the Caribbean as a whole or for larger parts; research organ of the Caribbean Commission.

Caribbean Quarterly (Port of Spain, Trinidad, University College of the West Indies), 1949–   . Quarterly. A general periodical devoted to West Indian art, history, folklore, and the like; the organ of the Extra-Mural Department of the University College.

The Daily Gleaner (Kingston, Jamaica), 1834–   . Jamaica's major daily newspaper. Also has a Sunday edition and (since 1951) a weekly overseas edition.

The Nation (Port of Spain, Trinidad), 1958–   . Weekly. Political newspaper; includes reprints of speeches, political commentary, and articles on the social and political history of Trinidad and Tobago.

Social and Economic Studies (Kingston, Jamaica, University College of the West Indies), 1953–   . Quarterly. Articles on social, economic, and political subjects, and scholarly papers on West Indian and other topics; the organ of the Institute of Social and Economic Research.

Trinidad Guardian (Port of Spain, Trinidad), 1918–   . Trinidad's major daily newspaper; also has a Sunday edition.

West Indian Economist (Kingston, Jamaica), 1958–   . Monthly. Political, economic, and social commentary.

West Indian Medical Journal (Kingston, Jamaica, University College of the West Indies), 1952–   . Articles on all aspects of medicine, sanitation, nutrition, and health services.

Index